Dealing with Demons

Insights into Evil Spiritual Influences and What to Do About Them

Selwyn R. Stevens, Ph.D.

Published by:

Jubilee
Resources International Inc.
Equipping Christians, Liberating Captives

Jubilee Resources International Inc.
PO Box 3, Feilding 4740, New Zealand

or our secure Internet Webshop at
www.jubileeresources.org

ISBN 978-1877463-12-9

All Scripture quotations in this book are from the New King James - New Authorised Version, unless otherwise noted.
Those marked CEV are from the Contemporary English Version
Those marked GW are from God's Word paraphrase
Those marked GNB are from the Good News Bible

The author uses American English spelling, not the Queen's English.

See order form on last page for this and other books which make a difference; especially the companion titles, "Dealing with Curses & Iniquities" and "The Bride Made Herself Ready." This book is about dealing with the less-powerful evil spirits or demons. When the reader wants to learn how to deal with the Principalities and Powers - the heavier-duty fallen angels - I would point you to my companion book, "The Bride Made Herself Ready" for that topic.

Acknowledgements:
Thanks to the teachings of the late Dr. Derek Prince, who has influenced multitudes over fifty years of teaching ministry. My thanks also go to my friends, Dr. Dale Sides, and the late Dr. Tom Hawkins, both of whom has provided me with much to think about relating to the spiritual realm. Also I wish to acknowledge the valuable teaching of the late Bill Subritzky, and the late Rev. Frank Marzullo Snr, from whom I have leaned much valuable and usable information for this ministry.

Contents

Introduction

The main reasons why Christians need to learn about demons are:

1. Because Jesus dealt with them, and told His disciples to do the same; and

2. To advance the Kingdom of God by setting people free from under all demonic influence and control.

> **"And He said to them, "Go into all the world and preach the gospel to every creature. "And these signs will follow those who believe: In My name they will cast out demons; they will speak with new tongues; "they will take up serpents; and if they drink anything deadly, it will by no means hurt them; they will lay hands on the sick, and they will recover." (Mark 16:15,17,18)**

This Scripture is addressed to believers in Jesus Christ, and He is stating those things that His Disciples - including us - should be doing. Wouldn't it be rebellious if we didn't do these things? What I don't understand is why more Christians aren't involved in this ministry when Jesus told us to do it. The enemy has hoodwinked too many in the church into neglecting this subject.

When a representative from a foreign government arrives in a country, they present their letters of authority, their credentials to the host country's authorities. Once they are accredited, they may then speak and act for those they represent. Christians are first and foremost Ambassadors for Christ. As such they have delegated authority to act in certain ways as Jesus has outlined in His teaching and ministry. Satan and the fallen angels and demons under his control must submit to every Disciple of Jesus Christ who has the indwelling Holy Spirit and who knows and uses the delegated authority given by Jesus. We have the power, the name and the blood of Jesus as our authority, and it is time we used it more effectively to set people free.

I trust the Lord will use this humble outline of how to advance the Kingdom of God for the glory of Jesus Christ, and the freedom of many. As we each are led by the Spirit of God, we will see Him move in power. It is a wonderful thing to see people set free from their bondages, curses and iniquities.

Selwyn Stevens
New Zealand

Chapter 1
The Spiritual Realm

We live in a spiritual world, whether or not we know it, or can understand it. The ultimate reality is God. The eternal Godhead is revealed in the Bible as Father, Son, and Holy Spirit (see 1 Timothy 3:16). God is the creator and alone is worthy of worship. (see Matthew 28:19-20; Colossians 1:16; 1 Peter 3:22; & Revelation 4:11). God is Spirit. A false understanding of the Godhead is one of the major belief of groups we usually call cults. Christians and Jews believe this statement in the Bible:

> **"Hear, Oh Israel: The LORD our GOD, The LORD is one." (Deut. 6:4)**

Even here we see the name of deity three times, so God is trying to show us something significant. For a wider look at the Christian doctrine of the tri-unity of God, I suggest you read the section in my books, "Holy Spirit Baptism & Filling," &"Essentials for Faith" where this topic is covered more fully than we have space here.

Angels

God has an everlasting kingdom and a divine order. (See Matthew 6:9-10; 2 Peter 1:11; Hebrews 12:28). All created beings began their existence to fulfil the will of God, according to:

> **"For by Him all things were created; things in heaven and on earth, visible and invisible, whether thrones or powers or rulers or authorities; all things were created by Him and for Him." (Colossians 1:16 NIV)**

These include angels, both God's and Fallen ones. These are powerful spiritual beings. The Hebrew word is "malak" meaning 'an agent or messenger;' and the Greek term "angelos" also means 'messenger.' All were created by God. There are both good and evil angels (the latter rebelled with Satan). Both groups come in various ranks of seniority.

First in importance and power are Archangels. Only two are mentioned in the Bible.

Michael - meaning "Who is like God." Michael's chief activities are to watch over the people of Israel, to war against Satan, and he is also involved in resurrection of the body. (Some religious groups, such as Jehovah's Witnesses and Seventh Day Adventists, have claimed that Jesus was actually Michael. This false belief cannot be sustained by Scripture.)

Gabriel - meaning "strength of God." Gabriel is the prophetic archangel. Since he is the Messenger of the One True God, claims that he appeared to Mohammed (the founder of Islam) are untrue, as angels sent by the One True God - the God of Abraham, Isaac and Ishmael - cannot bring false teaching.

There are angelic hosts, the elect angels who worship and serve God. (See Daniel 7:9-10; Matthew 26:53; Luke 2:13; Hebrews 12:22; Revelation 5:11).

The elect angels are the two-thirds who didn't follow Lucifer in his rebellion. The remaining third are fallen angels who fell by the sin of self-will: they chose to disobey God. God's loyal angels are controlled by Him, and are concerned with our welfare. Angels are never ours to command, or to seek communication with directly. Those who do seek such communication would be guilty of mediumship. In Scripture, the angels do interact with human beings, but they initiate the contact under God's orders, not from the humans. Great care is needed here.

According to Scripture, there appear to be seven orders or groups of angels.

Cherubim (Ezekiel 28:14; Job 1:6; 2:1) Assigned to the Heaven of Heavens. They protect areas to which they are assigned (Ark of Covenant, Tree of Life, etc.).

Seraphim (Isaiah 6:2,6) Assigned to the Heaven of Heavens. They protect the throne, testify to God's holiness, and are also worshippers.

Living Creatures (Ezekiel 1:5-6, 19) Assigned to the Heaven of Heavens. They protect the movement of holy things.

Worshipping Spirits (Rev. 5:11; 7:11; Luke 2:13-14) Primarily assigned to the Heaven of Heavens, but can appear on earth as directed. They have a function of worship before the throne of God.

Watchers (Genesis 6:2, 4; Jude 6) Were assigned to earth. They watched over and instructed mankind. They were corrupted by lust and left their first estate. They are chained in Tartarus.

Archangels (Daniel 10:13; 21; Jude 9) Assigned to earth and earth's atmosphere. They carry out orders to build the kingdom of God on earth. They have access to and from the heaven of heavens and may serve as emissaries to earth, on God's instructions.

Ministering Spirits (Daniel 10:11, 18; 1 Kings 19:7; Matt. 4:11; Mark 1:13; Heb. 1:7,14) Assigned to earth and earth's atmosphere. They are primary servants who carry out spiritual directives in warfare by God. They are assigned to people to help them accomplish what the Lord has authorised them to do.

Since God directs angels to do His bidding, we can petition God for angelic assistance, and then we should trust that God will instruct them according to His will. He is, after all, concerned for our best interests, provided these coincide with His plans and purposes.

Psalm 82:1 shows that there is a "Heavenly Council" consisting of both good and evil Celestial Beings, from which God takes advice and makes final decisions. Some are on God's right hand side (the righteous ones), and some on the left (the wicked). This is borne out in part in 2 Chronicles 18:18-22 with the lying spirit offering to entice King Ahab to his death.

Human Beings

Human Beings are triune beings too. We have a Spirit which provides "God-consciousness," the ability to communicate with God.; we have a Soul which provides "Self-consciousness," or the ability to be a person and have personality; and we have a Body which provides "us with World-consciousness" or the ability through the senses to understand. Our spirit changes kingdoms on salvation, but the battle ground remains our soul.

Lucifer/the Devil

God's most significant opponent was once in a position of power. Lucifer is a created anointed Cherub, and his name means "the Light-bearer" or "son of the morning." Originally he was the leader of worship of God, until pride and rebellion were found in his heart, and he was expelled from God's heaven. From then on, he is known as "the satan," meaning the accuser, (Ezekiel 28:14).

God the Creator is loving, benevolent and holy (meaning incapable of sin or evil). Evil cannot have originated with God, but came instead from Lucifer/the satan. "Satan" is not a real name, as it would be more accurate to describe him/it as the Adversary or Accuser. The "Devil" was expelled by God for rebellion against Him. The fallen angels that were expelled with Satan only constitute one-third of the angels God created. Since angels are created beings which cannot die, God created Hell as a place to keep all the fallen angels imprisoned for eternity. Hell was never originally intended as a place for human beings. Any human who ends up there does so by choice as a consequence of unrepentant rebellion against God.

Some people have a distorted idea of what the Devil looks like. He does not have horns, carry a trident and wear a red boiler suit. I heard one preacher describe him as a well-dressed used-car salesman. Whatever his appearance, it is clear he can sell human beings something that is bad for them and yet he makes it seem so attractive. Eve was certainly seduced into wanting something she didn't need, that cost her and the rest of us a great deal.

Let us be careful not to glorify the Devil or inflate his importance or power with too much attention. God and the Devil are not equals in power or persuasion. It is important we know that the Devil is NOT omnipresent, omnipotent or omniscient as God is. The Devil has to delegate much to Principalities and Powers as well as to the lowest in his structure, the demons.

The primary activities of the Devil are:
* TO tempt (see Matthew 4:1-11; Mark 1:13; Luke 4:1-13; 1 Corinthians 7:5; John 14:30; 1 John 5:18).
* TO deceive (Genesis 3:1-4, 13; 2 Corinthians 11:2-10; 1 Timothy 2:14; John 8;44; Ephesians 6:11 etc.)
* TO accuse (Revelation 12:10; Job 9-12; Zechariah 3:1-2)
* TO afflict (1 Corinthians 5:5; Luke 13:16; 2 Corinthians 12:7)
* TO oppose God and His purposes (1 Chronicles 21:1; Acts 10:38; Revelation 2:10; 12:4, 13,17; 13:7; 1 Thessalonians 2:18; 1 Peter 5:8; 2 Timothy 2:25-26).
* TO bring death (Hebrews 2:14; Jude 9; 1 John 3:12; John 8:44).

Under the Devil's control (but within the limits set by God - see Job 1:12), there are Principalities, Powers, Authorities, and Rulers.

> **"Put on the whole armor of God, that you may be able to stand against the wiles of the devil. For we do not wrestle against flesh and blood, but against principalities, against powers, against the rulers of the darkness of this age, against spiritual hosts of wickedness in the heavenly places." (Ephesians 6:11-12)**

Some of these seek to rule over nations, religions, people groups, denominations, churches and families.

Author Neil Anderson stated this well when he wrote, "How do you think Satan carries on his worldwide ministry of evil and deception? He is a created being. He is not omnipresent, omniscient, or omnipotent. He cannot be everywhere in the world tempting and deceiving millions of people at the same moment. He does so through an army of emissaries (demons, evil spirits, fallen angels, etc.) who propagate his plan of rebellion around the world. It is clear from the context of Ephesians 6:12 that the rulers, powers and forces which oppose us are spiritual entities in the heavenlies, in the spirit realm, in the spirit world." ("Daily Devotional" by Dr. Neil Anderson, www.devotional.crosswalk.com)

Fallen Angels

Fallen angels are not the same as demons or evil spirits. Many of the fallen angels were thrown into Hades - a prison for spirits, (2 Peter 2:4) and some were bound in chains of darkness (Jude 6). The saints (Christian believers) will judge the angels - meaning those that have fallen (1 Corinthians 6:3), and along with the Devil they will one day be cast into the Lake of Fire (Matthew 25:41; 2 Peter 2:4; Jude 6; Revelation 20:10).

Fallen angels are capable of embodiment, but don't seem to seek it. With the exception of the Devil entering Judas on the night of the betrayal of Jesus, there is no evidence of a fallen angel seeking to inhabit, or be limited within, a human body.

Demons or Evil Spirits

Demons are spiritual beings of a low order. Demons have personality, are able to think, act and speak. They are the slaves of the Devil - within the limits God permits them to act. They are probably the offspring of:

"the sons of God and the daughters of men" (Genesis 6:1)

Demons crave a human body to inhabit and through that they work out their desires. They are earthbound, which is their normal habitation. When not engaged in activity within a human being, it appears they dwell beneath the surface of the earth. Their gateways or portals into the human world are through geographic places where there has been repetitive sin practised, such as occult and pagan temples, where Masonic and other satanic rituals are performed. These can also be through human beings who are sold out to evil.

Every culture and religious faith on earth has some belief in evil spirits.

Animists, followers of Voodoo, Santaria and others live in constant fear of such spirits, and frequently offer sacrifices to placate them. Hinduism never questions the origins of evil spirits, but instead elevates them as gods. Most Buddhists think of demons as reincarnated spirits of dead humans. Greek and other ancient mythologies thought evil spirits were the offspring of Zeus or some other pagan deity.

Some people, including a few ministers who describe themselves as "Christian" don't actually believe there is a devil or any such thing as an evil spirit. This view puts them in profound opposition with Jesus Christ and the Holy Bible. Such people are already under the strong influence of the Spirit of the Anti-Christ - the spiritual principality that opposes Christ.

There are two mistakes possible when considering the demonic realm. First is a denial of its existence (and such blindness will prove to be futile and costly in time); and secondly some have an unhealthy interest in the demonic realm. These folks may be described as "Spook-Chasers," and their obsession is corrosive to a balanced Christian lifestyle.

Demons are not actually very powerful, and any Christian walking in their delegated authority from Jesus Christ, (see Mark 16:15-20) should have no difficulty in removing them from any repentant person.

Some people use terms such as "devils" (in the plural) and "demons," interchangeably. This is Biblically incorrect. Vines notes the noun "Diamon" meaning a demon signified among pagan Greeks an 'inferior deity, whether good or bad.' In the N.T. it denotes an evil spirit. It is used in Matthew 8:31 where it is mistranslated as "devils."

A second term "Diamonion" ...is also mistranslated "devil" or "devils." Vines goes on the note: "Demons are the spiritual agents acting in all idolatry. The idol itself is nothing, but every idol has a demon associated with it who induces idolatry with its worship and sacrifices (1 Corinthians 10:20-21; Revelation 9:20; & Deuteronomy 32:17; etc.)"

Vines also records a verb "Daimonizomi" signifies to be possessed by a demon, to act under the control of a demon." This term is widely understood to imply "demonized" as in 'influence' rather than 'possessed and under total control.'

Chapter 2
Where did Demons Originate?

There is a mystery about demons, or evil spirits, including their origin, function and interactions with human beings. Their identity and purpose have been deliberately obscured and the complexity of the "demonic enigma" should help us to understand them as creatures of deception.

There are hints in Scripture that suggest possibilities. Having checked a number of sources with diverse views, I noticed similarities by many Bible scholars regarding this matter. Let us look at two quotations.

Dr. Derek Prince writes, *"I have heard two main theories concerning the origin of demons.*
1. They are some of the fallen angels associated with [the] Satan in his rebellion against God. or;
2. They are disembodied spirits of a pre-Adamic race that perished under some judgment of God not recorded in detail in Scripture.

"I do not believe that Scripture provides us with sufficient evidence to say with certainty which, if either, of these theories is correct. I must say, however, that on the basis of my experience, I find it hard to believe that demons are fallen angels. It seems clear to me that even fallen angels still maintain their dwelling place somewhere in the "heavenly places" (Ephesians 6:12) - although not "in the third heaven" where God dwells (2 Corinthians 12:2-4). It is not scriptural, therefore, to represent angels as operating continually on the plane of the earth.

"Demons, on the other hand, appear to be earthbound creatures. Demons, as I have encountered them, display a wide range of character traits. Some are vicious, violent, supernaturally strong. Others are weak, cowering, even ridiculous - characteristics one would not expect to find in angels, even when they are fallen." ("They Shall Expel Demons" by Dr. Derek Prince, p. 91, DPM)

Dr. Kevin Conner describes three primary options of the origins of demons.

"1. That they were angels who fell with [the] Satan, some of which are bound while others are still loose (Psalm 78:49);

2. That they are disembodied spirits of a pre-Adamic race of beings, or some similar creation who fell when [the] Satan and his angels fell;

3. That they are the spirits of the unnatural offspring of angels (the Sons of God) and the antediluvian women in the days of Noah, (Genesis 6:1-6)." "Foundations of Christian Doctrine," by Kevin J. Conner B.Th., M.Div., Th.D (Hons) p. 109.)

Dr. Connor goes on to explain that while the Bible is silent on the specific origins of demons, it *"reveals them to be real personalities able to think, act and speak, and especially desiring to express themselves through mankind."*

For the sake of space, let me summarize the most widely-held view by most Bible scholars and theologians.

As the result of The Fall by Adam and Eve, recorded in Genesis 3:15, part of God's judgement against the Devil was that his ultimate nemesis would come through a Messiah with an undisclosed human lineage (described as "the seed of the woman"). Both Scripture and history have shown various attempts by the Devil to corrupt the bloodline of humanity. Genesis 6:1-4 describes the "Sons of God" having sexual relationships with the "daughters of men," resulting in offspring which were described as giants or Nephilim. The term "Sons of God" can only reliably describe angels (the fallen ones). Only from John 1:12 onward are human beings described as "sons of God" - the proviso being these must be Born Again into the Body of Christ. This is a New Testament concept not found in the Old Testament. All O.T. references to "Sons of God" in both context and translation refer to angelic beings.

Jude 6 and 7 refers to angels and sodomites from Sodom and Gomorrah as going after "strange flesh," which resulted in God's anger and judgement. While we cannot be certain beyond all doubt, it is possible only the family line of Noah were untouched by this crossbreeding between fallen angels and women, so God decided to wipe out everyone and start again with Noah's family and his ark full of preserved pairs.

When all flesh was drowned by the flood, the spirits of the hybrids couldn't go where human spirits went on death prior to Calvary. Consequently they remained in spirit form but were compelled to seek human flesh in which to dwell and operate.

There has been interesting research and writing about the controversial subject of UFO's that show reasonable grounds that the little green men associated with UFO's are actually demons. Many "alien" abductions include sexual abuse with attempts to impregnate or crossbreed. This tends to support such a possibility of demonic "space aliens." Space limitations and the need to stick to our subject prevent a more full coverage of that discussion here, despite fairly compelling evidence for such a link.

Let me here make a note of caution. Christians must be careful not to become absorbed and diverted from the call of our Lord Jesus Christ to be His Ambassadors, and to get on with evangelism, discipling, healing and being the salt and light for Christ in a hurting and needy world. There are too many ear-ticklers around with fanciful theories for which we cannot know the answers with any certainty. Since we weren't there, we must be careful not to become too dogmatic about these issues. The above is the most likely possibility from the evidence available, and the most widely agreed view of many Bible scholars. This is not a salvation issue, so differing views are okay without affecting our salvation. I am attempting to explain possibilities of the origins of demons from both reputable and other sources. I still have some questions regarding the views expressed above, and I also recognize much greater doubts attached to other opinions previously published. I am of the view we may never have a firm and incontrovertible answer to this dilemma until the Lord returns, and by then we may no longer be interested in the issue.

Regardless of their origins, demons are malevolent and evil spiritual beings that need a willing human body through whom to gratify their sinful nature. We humans are far better without them, and should seek their expulsion from us at the quickest possibility.

As Christians we have been told that
*	We aren't to be ignorant of the Devil's devices, agents & methods - 2 Corinthians 2:11;
*	We are called to be "Soldiers of the Lord" - 2 Timothy 2:3;
*	We are (knowingly or unknowingly) actively wrestling with these unseen forces - Ephesians 6:12;
*	Christians are to engage the enemy in this spiritual battle - Ephesians 2:2;
*	And to overcome him (Luke 10:19; Revelation 3:21).

Chapter 3
How do Demons operate?

Demons seek to fulfil their various lusts and appetites. Here are some spirits named in the Bible, showing their titles since these are their primary focus of activity. You will notice they are called by their effects rather than a personal name. That means these are verbs, not nouns.

Name given	Scripture Reference
• Unclean Spirit	Mark 7:25
• Spirit Of Falsehood	1 John 4:6
• Spirit Of Harlotry	Hosea 4:12
• Spirit Of Divination	Acts 16:16
• Haughty Spirit	Proverbs 16:18-19
• Lying Spirit	2 Chronicles 18:18-22
• Perverse Spirit	Isaiah 19:13-14
• Spirit Of Error	1 Tim. 4:1; 1 John 4:6
• Spirit Of Jealousy	Numbers 5:12-14
• Spirit Of Heaviness	Isaiah 61:1-3
• Spirit Of Bondage	Romans 8:15
• Spirit Of Sickness	Luke 5:15
• Deaf And Dumb Spirit	Mark 9:25-26
• Spirit Of Infirmity	Luke 13:11-16; Matt. 8:16-17
• Tormenting Spirits	Revelation 9:7-11
• Spirits Of Fear	Jer. 20:3b; 2 Tim. 1:7; Rom. 8:15
• Deceiving Spirits	1 Timothy 4:1-3, Gal. 3:1
• Spirit Of Deep Sleep	Isaiah 29:9-10
• Spirit Of Stupor	Romans 11:8
• Spirit Of Antichrist	1 John 4:2-3
• Spirit Of Death	Mark 9:22
• Religious Spirits	2 Kings 18:4
• Distressing Spirit	1 Samuel 16:14
• Familiar Spirits	1 Sam. 28:3,8,9; Deut. 18:11; Is. 8:19

There are some misguided people who declare that there have been no demons on earth since Calvary. Where did they go, and why do so many people these days have the symptoms of demon infestation? I believe the mass disappearance of demons and everything evil is still to happen!

The primary work of Demons is shown in the Bible as follows:

- To oppose God's ministers (Matthew 13:19; 2 Corinthians 4:4),
- To pervert the Word of God and seek to hinder the gospel (1 Thessalonians 2:18),
- They blind the minds of unbelievers (2 Corinthians 4:4),
- They seduce, corrupt, defraud and entice people (1 Timothy 4:1; Mark 13:22; 1 John 2:26),
- They trouble and torment people, to make them fearful (1 Chronicles 10:13-14; 2 Timothy 1:7; 1 John 4:18),
- They oppress people (Acts 10:38),
- They harass or molest people (Matthew 15:22; 17:15; Luke 6:18; Acts 5:16),
- They bind people (Luke 13:16),
- They deceive people (Revelation 12:9; Matthew 24:4,5,11,24),
- They defile people (Titus 1:15),
- They possess people - both in occupancy and ownership; (Matthew 4:24; 8:16, 28-34; Mark 5:1-20; Luke 8:26-39; Acts 8:7, 16:16).

One of my country's most well-known experts in this subject, Bill Subritzky, wrote about his experiences on demons, *"They fight against our personal harmony, our peace of mind and physical well-being, causing disruptiveness with other people, especially those closest to us. Their great distinctive mark is restlessness.*

They can affect us in our emotions, attitudes and relationships, for example they cause resentment, hatred, fear or rebellion.

In addition they can affect the thoughts of the mind, causing doubt, unbelief, indecision and procrastination.

In the area of the tongue, they can cause lying, cursing, gossip and blasphemy, and in the sexual area, perversion, homosexuality and masturbation.

Further, they can affect us in the areas of alcohol, nicotine, gluttony and anorexia and in physical infirmities they often cause tumors, heart attacks, arthritis, allergies and cramps.

Most addictions come out of frustration.

The demon of lying needs a tongue to lie through, a demon of doubt needs a mind to doubt through, and a demon of lust needs sexual organs to lust through.

If we have recurrent evil, disruptive, emotional attitudes which dominate us against our will, for example resentment, hatred, fear, jealousy, and pride or extreme moodiness with changes from being extremely talkative to unnaturally quiet, or if there is an unnatural restlessness and talkativeness, these can be signs of demonic activity." ("How to Cast Out Demons and Break Curses," by Bill Subritzky, p 14-15 Dove).

Let us check out some Scriptures that outline how demons function.

> **"...as well as those who were tormented with unclean spirits. And they were healed," (Luke 6:18).**
>
> **"Also a multitude gathered from the surrounding cities to Jerusalem, bringing sick people and those who were tormented by unclean spirits, and they were all healed," (Acts 5:16).**
>
> **"So ought not this woman, being a daughter of Abraham, whom Satan has bound for eighteen years, be loosed from this bond on the Sabbath?" (Luke 13:16).**
>
> **"For unclean spirits, crying with a loud voice, came out of many who were possessed; and many who were paralysed and lame were healed. 16) Now it happened, as we went to prayer, that a certain slave girl possessed with a spirit of**

divination met us, who brought her masters much profit by fortune-telling," (Acts 8:7; 16)

"Therefore we wanted to come to you - even I, Paul, time and again - but Satan hindered us," (1 Thessalonians 2:18).

"...whose minds the god of this age has blinded, who do not believe, lest the light of the gospel of the glory of Christ, who is the image of God, should shine on them," (2 Corinthians 4:4).

"Now the Spirit expressly says that in latter times some will depart from the faith, giving heed to deceiving spirits and doctrines of demons," (1 Timothy 4:1).

"...how God anointed Jesus of Nazareth with the Holy Spirit and with power, who went about doing good and healing all who were oppressed by the devil, for God was with Him," (Acts 10:38).

"As they went out, behold, they brought to Him a man, mute and demon-possessed. And when the demon was cast out, the mute spoke. And the multitudes marvelled, saying, "It was never seen like this in Israel!" (Matthew 9:32-33).

Let's not go overboard with this fact, but 24% of the verses about the ministry of Jesus were to do with Him evicting demons from people. Every effective minister of the Gospel and every disciple involved in the healing ministry will come across demons from time to time.

The point can be sustained, both from the Bible as well as wide experience, that many sicknesses and afflictions are caused by the demonic realm, or evil spirits. You must also understand that not every sickness is demonic in origin, so wisdom and discernment must be utilized.

Here are some more relevant Scriptures about dealing with demons:

> **"When Jesus saw that the people came running together, He rebuked the unclean spirit, saying to it, "Deaf and dumb spirit, I command you, come out of him and enter him no more!" (Mark 9:25).**

We need to know the following:

1. Demons have knowledge of the deity, authority, and power of the Lord Jesus Christ, according to Mark 1:24; 3:11; 5:7; Luke 4:41; and Acts 19:15.

2. Demons fear their future judgement and confinement in the Abyss, according the Luke 8:28,31.

3. Demons showed that Jesus Christ had total authority over them on earth, because they obeyed every command He gave them, according to Matthew 8:31, 32; Mark 1:25.

4. Demons still fear and obey the name of Jesus Christ when it is used in faith, according to Mark 16:17; Acts 8:5-7; 16:18.

In light of these, demons submit to the authority of the One who conquered them. Since all Disciples of Jesus Christ have been given delegated authority over demons, freedom from evil influences can be obtained by those who use the power and authority given us by our Lord Jesus Christ.

Chapter 4
How Might We Get Demonized?

First and foremost, sin opens the doorway. With our own lips we might utter a self-curse, a rash vow or similar (see the companion book, "Dealing with Curses & Iniquities" to explain these). These permit a demon to have a legal right of entry. Attitudes such as unforgiveness, resentment and bitterness can also provide a legal entry-point, as can involvement in the Occult, including Wicca, witchcraft of all types, the making of ungodly covenants such as in Freemasonry and many other lodges, and any type of idolatry.

Some children, even as yet unborn, have been known to be dedicated to the Devil, or to one of his public faces such as pagan deities. God pronounces iniquity on to the third and fourth generation for sins such as idolatry, and to ten generations for sexual sins.

Along with many others in ministry, I have found that the most demonized people are those who won't come under proper Biblical authority.

Familiar spirits are well-known among those with Bible-based deliverance ministries. The King James Version uses the term "Familiar Spirit" sixteen times and it usually refers to a spirit of divination or its medium (the person through whom it operates). In the Hebrew, 'familiar' means a "Knowing Spirit." These particular spirits are familiar with a family and seek to influence it generation after generation. It knows the weaknesses physically, mentally, spiritually and emotionally. These don't get Alzheimer's disease, so they never forget anything. Most people with so-called "Psychic" powers actually have a familiar spirit operating through them.

Vito Rallo states, *"A familiar spirit is familiar with an individual or family's sins. It knows what buttons to push on each family member. It knows every weakness and most every thing about that family member, in order to influence each of them to sin, and the curse is passed on. This familiar spirit may have been with a family for generations and can be passed on to future generations who also sin, which allows the same spirit to transcend several generations.*

For example, if your father or mother was an alcoholic or drug abuser, those evil spirits will watch you. They know that you probably already inherited a weakness for alcohol or drugs, and they will drive you crazy. If you have children, they will be ready to attack them, too. They try to get each generation involved in the same sin, so they can carry the curse on and on. These spirits that control the parents frequently control the children, and many times, the manifestations of the stronghold are much worse in the succeeding generations. Their control can grow with each passing generation.

The Old Testament warns about familiar spirits. Leviticus 19:31 says, "Give no regard to mediums and familiar spirits; do not seek after them, to be defiled by them: I am the Lord your God." Leviticus 20:6 reads, "And the person who turns to mediums and familiar spirits, to prostitute himself with them, I will set My face against that person and cut him off from his people."

Many people consult mediums, clairvoyants, and spirits to gain knowledge about the future. They think they are receiving information from the spirit of a loved one or from the spirit of a person who has passed from this life to death. One cannot call up a spirit of a deceased person. (No one can except Jesus Christ Himself.) That spirit that has been conjured up by someone in the occult practice of necromancy is an evil, lying spirit. It may know things about the past, but it can't predict the future. It may know things about you or your circumstances, but that is what a familiar spirit is all about. It will give you enough truth to hook you into thinking it is good, and then fill you with lies to destroy you. There is no such thing as a "good" familiar spirit.

Note: A familiar spirit may enter a person through his or her involvement in occult practices, condemning that person by his or her own actions. Many of the ills of our society are caused by the involvement in occult practices, i.e. witchcraft, fortune-tellers, psychics, etc. These practices open the door to a life that is subject to numerous strongholds/curses. Disobedience opens the door." ("Breaking Generational Curses and Pulling Down Strongholds" by Vito Rallo, pps 36-37)

I am pleased Vito stated "There is no such thing as a "good" familiar spirit." According to the official Mormon/Latter-day Saints publication, *"A Marvellous Work and a Wonder,"* pages 67-68, every copy of the "Book of Mormon" has a Familiar Spirit prayed into it, for the express purpose of deceiving the reader into the belief that the book contains truth rather than error. I encourage people to send the evil spirit to its appointed place to await judgement, and then burn the book since it is only a fairy story with a few extracts from the Bible added to pretend it is authentic.

Dr. Dale Sides wrote a very incisive investigation on demons. Let us consider the following quotation from his article.

> **"And they (the people) were astonished at His (Jesus') teaching, for His word was with authority. Now in the synagogue there was a man who had a spirit of an unclean demon. And he cried out with a loud voice: saying "Let us alone! What have we to do with You Jesus of Nazareth? Did You come to destroy us? I know You, who You are - the Holy One of God!" But Jesus rebuked him, saying, "Be quiet, and come out of him!" And when the demon had thrown him in their midst, it came out of him and did not hurt him," (Luke 4:32-35).**

From this passage we see:

1. Demons do not like authoritative people. They usually do not manifest in the first person unless around an authoritative person or when confronted by a person who knows their identity.

2. They are spirits who can live in the bodies of men or women. They do not have their own flesh and bone body (Luke 24:39).

3. They are unclean, meaning that they are not holy and are filthy in habit. This indicates that uncleanness is one of the criteria they seek in a host.

4. Demons also have a will which is exhibited by the fact that the unclean demon spirit cries out.

5. They do not want to be bothered but can lie dormant until discovered.

6. They have an end, meaning they can and will be destroyed.

7. They are under authority to Jesus and His disciples.

8. They go to church and like to occupy religious people who are ignorant of their methods. ("Episkopos" magazine, by Dr. Dale Sides, Oct. 1999, p 3)

Levels of Demonic Influence and Activity

1. Temptation. (e.g. 1 Corinthians 10:13) We all are!

2. Harassment, such as Paul's thorn in the flesh (2 Corinthians 12:7). The main signs include sickness, emotional disturbance, physical infirmity, etc. This is where most Christians will minister.

3. Inhabitation. An example would include the Demoniac at the Gadarenes (Mark 5:1-10)

It doesn't matter whether they are "in," "on," or whatever - just get rid of them! There is too much useless debate about demons, and too many people are "counseling" demons. Jesus said to cast them out!

Please note: the original Greek text of the New Testament never speaks of people being "possessed" or "owned" by demons. A more accurate translation would be "demonized," "afflicted" or "harassed" by demons. A person who is born again by the Spirit of God cannot be "possessed" by a demon, but can be "oppressed" or "afflicted" by one. The issue is ownership, and Christians are bought with a price by Jesus at Calvary. A true Christian is "possessed" by Jesus Christ.

When Jesus ministered He used few words.

> **"And He cast out the spirits with a word, and healed all who were sick," (Matthew 8:16).**

There are two main questions to ask people who want ministry;

Firstly - Do you really want to be free?

Secondly - Are you willing to do what it takes to get and stay free?

I am no longer surprised at the number of people who are brought to our center for ministry, especially deliverance issues, by family members and friends. These well-meaning folk frequently haven't asked if the person requiring ministry actually wants it. We have learned to ask that question very early on as many are honest in their response - NO! Doing ministry against someone's will is wrong and won't work. It is just a waste of time and since there is a queue of people who really do want to be free, it seems better stewardship of our time to be certain the person actually wants ministry before trying to do any. If their will is not engaged in such ministry, we will achieve nothing but exhaustion for all concerned. Satan and the demons would be very happy with a situation where Christians get so worn down doing ministry that they do something wrong and embarrass the Kingdom of God. If the person is not willing to participate in their own freedom from evil spirits, we tell them to go away and return only when they are willing. We have others waiting who really do want their freedom.

Demons are morally unclean, according to Matthew 10:1; Mark 1:27; Romans 6:13; Luke 8:27 and elsewhere. As disciples of the Lord Jesus Christ, we have the authority to command demonic spirits to leave. There should be little difficulty in doing so, provided the legal ground which allowed them in the first place has been dealt with. Some people seem to love watching others manifest wildly, that does nothing for their dignity. Personally the moment there is any sign of a manifestation, I bind and prevent them from doing that, commanding them to go immediately. If they will not go immediately, I stop the ministry and ask the Lord, and often the person if there is any remaining legal ground for the demon to stand on. We need to deal with that before moving on.

> **"For though we walk in the flesh, we do not war according to the flesh. For the weapons of our warfare are not carnal but mighty in God for pulling down strongholds, casting down arguments and every high thing that exalts itself against the knowledge of God, bringing every thought captive to the obedience of Christ." (2 Corinthians 10: 3-5)**

Dr. Grant Mullen M.D., a Christian medical doctor specializing in mood disorders including depression, writes:

"Spiritual attack is a very real issue, especially in depressed Christians. The loss of concentration and the cluttering of negative thoughts make a person particularly vulnerable to occult influences. When a person's mind is filled with negative discouraging thoughts that can't be shut off, then it is very easy for Satan to insert even more condemning thoughts or suggestions in among the person's own thoughts. The depressed person is unable to detect the intrusion of lies, condemnation or misinterpretations from an evil source and just assumes that the thoughts are his own. The inserted thoughts are intended to magnify the pain of depression and to separate the victim from supportive friends, counsellors and, most of all, from God. When concentration is impaired by depression, it is very difficult to "take every thought captive" and block the intrusion of dark thoughts. In my experience, the first step in the process of deliverance or becoming free from the harassment of evil is to treat any depression that may be present. When thought control and concentration is restored, then believers can use their authority over Satan and he will flee." (Moods: What Christians Should Know" by Dr. Grant Mullen pages 9-10,)

Jesus warned us in John 10:10 that Satan came to steal from us, kill and destroy us. Why does the Devil want to do that? The Devil seeks to attack us because he is unable to attack God directly - he lacks the ability and power. So he attacks God's people, using various guerrilla warfare methods. When the Devil attacks God's people, they often believe the lies about the Devil's power and start to withdraw from reaching people for Christ. If the Devil cannot get you on his side against God, he will seek to hinder you, to thwart God's purposes in your life, to make you ineffective. Most of the Devil's attacks are designed to cut us off from relationship with God so we will actively disbelieve God. The Devil attacks our minds so we become crippled in our emotions and in our relationships with God and each other.

But: 1 John 3:8 declares:

> **"The reason the Son of God appeared was to destroy the works of the devil."**

We are called into that same battle. We are not just to hold ground already taken, but we are to add to it by evangelism, healing, discipleship, etc. Sadly many of us are ill-prepared by our churches and pastors to mature into such a God-commanded role.

Exorcism

The deliverance ministry is sometimes called "exorcism," although that is an occultic ritual found in many ancient magical texts, and adopted erroneously by the Roman Catholic Church and some others. *"The only 'exorcists' in the Bible tried to use the name of Jesus in a magical way without being truly saved. Thus they had no authority. They got the tar beaten out of them by a demon-possessed man (see Acts 19:13-19)."* ("Blood on the Doorposts" by William and Sharon Schnoebelen, Chick Publications, p 332)

Exorcism involves suppressing the symptoms caused by one demon by putting a stronger demon to control the weaker one. That isn't freedom, and it certainly is not Biblical. Genuine Christians do not do "exorcisms" for this reason.

Ministry without Repentance

This is pointless, according to Jesus. In Matthew 12:43-45, Jesus speaks about an unclean spirit that had left a person, but not finding a better place to dwell (having a legal right to re-enter the person) the unclean or demonic spirit returns and brings seven worse spirits, compounding the problems of that person.

> **"When an evil spirit comes out of a man, it goes through arid places seeking rest and does not find it. Then it says,**

> **"I will return to the house I left." When it arrives it finds the house unoccupied, swept clean and put in order. Then it goes and takes with it seven other spirits more wicked than itself, and they go and live there. And the final condition of the man is worse than the first" (Matthew 12:43-45)**

If a person won't renounce a legal ground for oppression, then the ministry is over until they do, as we don't want them seven times worse. It is a failure of those leading such ministry that can put people into mental hospitals with severe depression, suicide attempts and the like. It is time for much better balance of teaching and ministry in this area. I have seen some horrific ministry done in the name of Jesus by people way out of their depth, and far beyond their ability to achieve freedom for the person requiring ministry. Sometimes is comes from ignorance of their authority in Christ; and other times it is guesswork and presumption without wisdom or true knowledge of Godly authority.

We should discourage people from seeking deliverance from an evil spirit until they are willing to renounce the sin that gives it legal ground to be there. I don't want that person needing freedom from several more spirits because we didn't get it right the first time.

Dignity

The dignity of the person receiving ministry is very important. Don't forget to retain your own dignity too, for this isn't to entertain or provide a sideshow. We are ambassadors for Christ, and all Ambassadors do things with a certain dignity and decorum, especially in Jesus' name! Name the problem - it is not essential to name the demon or to know it's name. It is more important to name its function what it does. Then tell it to go "In the name of Jesus Christ of Nazareth." Please note: casting a demonic spirit out is not a polite request, but rather an authoritative command.

Conversations with demons are never to be encouraged. There is no Biblical basis for trying to do so, although our team have met some who do teach and practice this. One has to twist Scriptures to say what they don't to believe this teaching. According to the Bible this is actually practicing Mediumship, a sin serious enough to keep you out of God's heaven for eternity.

So if a sickness is demonic in origin, then just command (Fever, Epilepsy, Cancer, Infirmity, Death... or whatever,) to go "in the name of Jesus Christ of Nazareth." Your authority to command evil spirits is from Jesus Himself, if you are His disciple.

> **"And these signs will follow those who believe: In My name they will cast out demons ..." (Mark 16:17)**

The question each of us should ask is, "What signs are following you?"

Where do or should Demons go?

Scripture mentions "Dry Places." What exactly does this mean? Without making it a "doctrine" I think it means the spirit is not permitted to re-enter a human or animal. A friend of mine who is a church Elder and who teaches high school science provided me with the following two references.

"99 out of 100 molecules in the body are water molecules. However, because water is much smaller and lighter than other molecules like proteins and fats, water contributes to about 60% of the total weight of a person." ("Human Physiology" by van der Sherman & Luciano. 2nd edition, McGraw Hill 1975)

"The average amount of water by weight in a human female is about 52%, but the average amount by weight in a human male is about 63%." (David Shier, Jackie Butler & Ricky Levy, pub. by McGraw Hill 1999)

Some people direct demons to "the foot of the cross," while others command them to go to "The appointed place." I'm not saying these are wrong, but they don't appear to have a Biblical basis. The important thing is that the evil spirits go, and don't return!

Rebuking with Authority

It is widely understood that the reference to serpents and scorpions in the following passage is actually about the demonic realm.

> **"Behold, I give you the authority to trample on serpents and scorpions, and over all the power of the enemy, and nothing shall by any means hurt you," (Luke 10:19).**

The facts are that we have authority delegated by Jesus to deal with the demonic spirits. We should not be fearful of them, for even if they threaten (and they often try to) they must submit to the authority, name and blood of Jesus Christ.

Prayer & Fasting

Prayer and fasting indicates a solid and safe relationship with God through the Lord Jesus Christ. It includes walking in humility rather than in pride. Jesus had to rebuke His disciples for their unbelief. Allowing that they were still learning ministry methods, Jesus wants us to minister out of relationship with Him through the Holy Spirit. Fasting involves humbling and disciplining our bodies for the service of God. There are many scriptures encouraging fasting.

I ministered with a woman in Kitwe in Zambia who was bent over just like the woman Jesus healed in Luke 13:11-13. One important point I wish to mention here - the woman I ministered with had given legal ground to the spirit of infirmity when she accepted herbs provided to her from a witchdoctor through her Pentecostal pastor. She was only healed once she renounced the herbs, the witchdoctor and his powers. She was freed and ran around the room upright in about one minute. The pastor interpreting for me was sent to her home to cleanse it of anything else from the witchdoctor, then went on to sort out the pastor who should have known better.

Speaking of Africa, during ministry following teaching, I was struck by the number who described their condition as "general body pain." This would have been the comment from over half those who came forward. Virtually all were caused by spirits of infirmity. Arthritis is often caused by unforgiveness; and many muscular problems such as Parkinsons Disease, Arthritis, Muscular Dystrophy, Chronic Fatigue/ Fibromyalgia etc. seem to be significantly caused by Freemasonry Curses. These conclusions are based on many years of practical experience.

Chapter 5
Prior to Ministry

• Check the person is saved. (John 3:16; 2 Corinthians 5:17)

• Check they have been baptized in water. Infant sprinkling, erroneously called "baptism" won't suffice, according to Scripture. Baptism requires prior repentance (Romans 6:4) whereas an infant doesn't know how to.

• Do they have the habit of daily prayer and Bible reading? This is essential if they are to grow in God and spiritual maturity. (Psalm 1:1-3; 1 Thessalonians 5:17)

• Do they attend a Bible-believing fellowship where mature Disciples of Jesus can minister to each other. (Hebrews 10:25)

• Do they have an attitude of Thanksgiving to God. (Philippians 4:6; Psalm 100:4)

• Do they have an attitude of forgiveness to others, (Matthew 6:9-14.)

Dealing with the Demonic

1. Crowd them out. Let Jesus and The Holy Spirit so fill our lives there is no space for the demons to occupy.

2. Starve them out. Demons can't handle chosen holiness. They feed on sin, unforgiveness etc., so remove their food through repentance. I liken this to rats at a rubbish dump. The rats are there because there is something to eat - food. If the food was removed, that rats would leave to find food elsewhere.

3. Command them out. We have authority, according to Jesus. Our failure to use our delegated authority is the main reason we have many of the problems we do have.

4. Stand Your Ground - God's Word is a sword -

> **"Therefore submit to God. Resist the devil and he will flee from you." (James 4:7)**

We need to resist the devil before he will flee. We can't resist him unless we are first submitted to God. Remember the KISS principle - Keep it simple, Saint!

> **"And He cast out the spirits with a word, and healed all who were sick." (Matthew 8:16)**

Common sense as well as discernment giftings should tell you that a broken arm is not a "Spirit of Broken Arm;" that a cut finger is not a demon of cut finger; and a burned leg is not a spirit of burned leg. Many people have accidents that cause blindness, deafness, and much more. Some are born with physical impairments. These have been known to have been caused by the mother's use of recreational or other drugs such as Thalidomide, Marijuana, Heroin, etc. Sometimes these can be attributed to Generational Iniquity issues (curses down family lines) even allergic reactions to chemicals and sprays used in orchards, war zones and much more. And Jesus loves these people too, and wants to heal them.

Not all conditions are caused by demons, but many can be. Use wisdom and discernment.

Anyone doing effective ministry will come across demons that need to be dealt with.

Chapter 6
Preparation For The Minister

Suggested Do's for the Minister of Deliverance

1. Go through deliverance yourself - first. (Matthew 10:8)

2. Get filled with the Holy Spirit, believing God for most, if not all, of the manifestations mentioned in 1 Corinthians 12. (Please see my companion book, "Holy Spirit - Baptism and Filling" for details on how to receive this.)

3. Be active in the other manifestations of the Holy Spirit. (Romans 12:6-8) Paul is tells us not to minister beyond the proportion of grace and faith that is given to us. That means we can also mature into these.

4. Ask the Holy Spirit to give you a servant's attitude, (Mark 10:43-44). Jesus is saying that we should learn to serve. Have a servant's heart and attitude.

5. Know that God has called you (all believers) into this ministry. (Mark 16:17) No exceptions are recorded in the Bible.

Suggested Don'ts for the Minister of Deliverance

1. Don't believe false concepts such as: "This is not my ministry."

2. Don't use pat answers; "I know just how you feel" or "give it all to Jesus." Most people, if they knew how to surrender their life to Christ, would not need your help.

3. Don't feel that you have to come up with the answer to everything. If you don't know, say so, but tell them that you will try to find out for them. Be faithful to get back to them about the question.

4. Don't try to cast out every possible demon or try to cover too much territory in one session. Keep sessions under two hours if at all possible. God's chosen people took the land God had given them little by little - as much as they were able to hold onto at a time.

5. Don't wear yourself out, or your prayer partner, or the counselee. The devil could take advantage of that. We try to minister when we are fresh in the morning if we can. We need to be fresh so that we can hear the Word of the Lord more clearly. Satan would like you to be tired and worn out. If there is an emergency, then we will minister deliverance as it is truly needed but not usually as it is demanded or even wanted.

6. Don't become a permanent crutch. Teach self-deliverance. Don't take the place of the Holy Spirit in the counselee's life especially if they want to lean on you and they don't hear Him enough. We have to teach people to be overcomers. We can not overcome for them. You can help them overcome up to a point, but then that person has to overcome by themselves.

7. Don't do anything contrary to scripture, such as "I'll take on your demon." You shouldn't want anyone else's demons!

8. Don't advise anything that presumes on God, such as "now throw away your pills." Let God or their doctor say they don't need medicine any more.

9. Don't reveal confidential information - to anyone. Get specific permission first from the counselee if you think you have a need to share someone's story with anyone. If authorities should be informed of a crime - warn the counselee of your legal and/or moral responsibility (such as in the case of continuing sexual abuse of a minor).

10. Don't counsel alone in a private place with a member of the opposite sex. Have a prayer partner with you. Our preferred method is that men should deliver men, and women should deliver women. Married couples make a good team if their relationship is solid in the Lord.

11. Be very careful about physical contact. Watch out for lust and loneliness. Spirits take advantage of lonely people.

12. Be careful of your personal hygiene, don't be sloppy in appearance, prevent body odour, bad breath, etc.

13. Don't minister if either of you are too tired. Be rested and filled with the Holy Spirit's peace and joy. Beware of the "messiah" complex. God can and will get His work done without you - He wants your obedience, not your sacrifices.

14. Don't think you can't fail yourself. Everyone can.

Chapter 7
Why Some Ministers Fail In Deliverance Work

1. They are immature. They are just too inexperienced in the ministry of deliverance. "...not a novice, lest being puffed up with pride he fall into the same condemnation as the devil. Moreover he must have a good testimony among those who are outside, lest he fall into reproach and the snare of the devil." (1 Timothy 3:6-7)

2. They are dirty vessels containing lust, gluttony, anger, bitterness etc. Can a person who is in adultery cast out demons? Yes, for the gifts and calling of God are irrevocable. A minister who harbors sin or if there are demonic influences in his/her own life, will be hindered by these in his ministry. It is not so much the gifts, but the fruit of the Holy Spirit that qualifies a minister of deliverance. If a person tries to cast out a spirit out of another, while he/she has the same spirit, it could intensify the problem for both of them.

3. The lack of Prayer, fasting and/or dependance on Holy Spirit. Note Matthew 17:21 "However, this kind does not go out except by prayer and fasting."

4. They become emotionally involved, taking on the person's burden.

5. They fall by their pride.

6. They use illegal techniques; e.g. the minister might be involved in controlling or manipulating the counselee.

7. The Minister and Counselee have similar weaknesses such as lust, divination, antichrist, witchcraft, etc.

8. Failure to be sure counselee has their necessary their foundationsin place, e.g. Repentance, Forgiveness based only on Christ's work,

Assurance of Salvation, Water Baptism, Embracing the Cross and Self-denial, Submission to Godly authority, etc. Just because a person says that he/she was born again does not mean they are. Is there fruit that gives evidence of repentance, of being born again, of self-denial and Cross bearing? The fruit of the Holy Spirit will unerringly tell us that the Tree of Life (Christ) is growing in a person's life.

9. They forget that the problem could have an organic cause. Such as improper nutrition, hormone imbalance, brain damage, etc. The body certainly needs proper nutrition and physical care to function correctly, and prayer for healing may be in order, rather than deliverance from a demon.

10. They neglected to observe the counselee was **insufficiently motivated to be free**, not willing to accept responsibilities of freedom, nor willing to give up everything to obey Jesus.

11. The counselee is blaming others for their condition; e.g. parents, spouse, anybody but themselves. They must take responsibility for their attitudes and all of their actions. No one can make us sin.

12. The Counselee is ignorant of or unskilled in the use of the Word of God. If we do not study God's word then we can neither know His will nor can we use it to defeat the enemy. **"Do your best to present yourself to God as one approved, a workman who does not need to be ashamed and who correctly handles the Word of Truth." (2 Timothy 2:15)**

Chapter 8
The Spirit of Religion

In Matthew 23, Jesus mentions the spirit of Religion by the description of how this works. Please look at this subject more closely, because this is one of the most significant causes preventing the work of the Holy Spirit in much of the Western church these days. (Much of my thinking on this topic has been expanded by Pastor Chris Hayward, President of Cleaning Streams.)

The Spirit of Religion must be confronted - it can never be left to control or manipulate the people of God, including those in leadership. It is bold, intimidating and ruthless, and it requires a bold, wise and strong leader to confront and deal with it.

While it will be painful and unpleasant at the time, personal and corporate growth and maturity will result from dealing with the Spirit of Religion.

If you compromise and allow it to prosper, you will grieve the Holy Spirit of God, and become frustrated with your inability to move forward into the things of God. The longer you wait until you confront and deal with it, the more entrenched it will become and the harder to get rid of. When Elijah confronted the prophets of Baal it was needful for a power confrontation. This may also be necessary when we confront the same spirit today.

Call the trusted believers together, and ask for wisdom, strength and God's strategy in this battle. Some people will seek to compromise because they want a quiet life. That isn't an option. It you want a quiet life now, you will have a terribly noisy eternity, complete with the "gnashing of teeth," but if you will be obedient to the Lord now, you will have a much quieter eternity.

My friend, Chris Hayward, states the order to protect and move forward as follows: *"Proclaim the Word of God, employ the power of the Cross, and begin to take authority over every demonic scheme that has been assigned to you. Give praise and thanksgiving to the One who is in you, and who is greater than anything that is coming against you. Pray - and then pray some more! Pray before you confront, pray while you confront, and pray after you confront.*" ("Freedom from the Religious Spirit" General Editor: Dr. C. Peter Wagner - Chapter by Chris Hayward p117.)

Matthew 23 is one of the best explanations about the workings of this spirit of religion. We learn that it is quick to use its victims to point out the failures and needs of others, while being totally blind to their own shortcomings.

For example, it often induces people to criticize others in areas they themselves are lacking in. (verse 3) They expect more from you than they do from themselves. They also fail to see your need for assistance with the burdens you are carrying. (Verse 4) Chris states that one of the first places the spirit of religion shows up is among those who seek recognition. Often subtle, it can be found among those seeking position, titles or power/control. (verse 5)

But God's recognition is all we really need, in His time and ways.

The spirit of religion causes people to seek recognition for what they do, and what they are. There is a false and inflated pride in their position or influence. The spirit of Religion will always seek to quench the work of the Holy Spirit. If the Holy Spirit is in control, then the spirit of Religion cannot be, and we cannot let it! Actually true followers of Jesus Christ do want the Holy Spirit in control, all the time, for it makes for an exciting and eventful life. This means breaking with some things from the past, such as church or family traditions. The founding families of some churches are particularly fond of seeking to prevent change because it looks like their family tradition is being ignored or devalued. But nothing is forever, except God, so change is a natural part of what we all face, whether we like it or not. In times of much change, like our lives these days, this can be a bit overwhelming for some. They seek to prevent all change, even beneficial change. Alvin Tofler wrote a book about this during the 1970's, called "Future Shock" and the issues are more relevant than ever.

Actually, on the issue of founding families being "ignored" etc., perhaps there is a need to more publicly recognize the benefits of those who have gone before, while acknowledging the need for updating things from time to time. Some of those situations, when handled carefully, could reduce the opportunity for the spirit of Religion to upset things through people. Wisdom and patience are essential ingredients for careful growth and maturity. The age-old issue of new and old wineskins, as mentioned by Jesus in Matthew 9:16-17, should show that some church structures cannot change enough to fit the newer needs of the people. Maybe a new wineskin needs to be designed and commenced so people can get on with Kingdom imperatives.

Demons never want to encourage God's purposes - their boss has instructed them to prevent anything God wants accomplished. The good news is that God wins and has His way, but He does allow Satan and his demons to buffet the people of God so we are battle-hardened, overcomers and victorious. Chris Hayward says accurately, (demons) will always seek to undermine any leader that attempts to bring the fresh wind of the presence of the Holy Spirit into the Body of Christ - the church. "Many a battle has been lost at this juncture," Chris states.

The spirit of Religion will:
Seek to gather people around the key person it is using.
It will seek ways to gain attention.
It will look for ways to subvert divine order.
It will seek to demean and slander legitimate authority.
It will claim it would be a better leader than those presently in authority.
It will pretend humility, while operating with pride.

It will major on minor issues, and minor on major issues. Tradition and image are everything. They are often impatient with church members in need, thinking they should have been more careful with their finances.

The spirit of Religion wants to remove the true prophets of God, because prophets point out the truth, regardless of consequences. True prophets want to build up God's people and do not seek to focus on themselves. Power and influence of spirits of Religion are undermined by true prophets of God.

Let's read from the CEV:

> **Jesus said to the crowds and to his disciples:**
>
> **The Pharisees and the teachers of the Law are experts in the Law of Moses.**
>
> **So obey everything they teach you, but don't do as they do. After all, they say one thing and do something else.**
>
> **They pile heavy burdens on people's shoulders and won't lift a finger to help.**
>
> **Everything they do is just to show off in front of others. They even make a big show of wearing Scripture verses on their foreheads and arms, and they wear big tassels for everyone to see.**
>
> **They love the best seats at banquets and the front seats in the meeting places.**
>
> **And when they are in the market, they like to have people greet them as their teachers.**
>
> **But none of you should be called a teacher. You have only one teacher, and all of you are like brothers and sisters.**
>
> **Don't call anyone on earth your father. All of you have the same Father in heaven.**
>
> **None of you should be called the leader. The Messiah is your only leader.**
>
> **Whoever is the greatest should be the servant of the others.**
>
> **If you put yourself above others, you will be put down. But if you humble yourself, you will be honoured.**
>
> **You Pharisees and teachers of the Law of Moses are in for trouble! You're nothing but show-offs. You lock people out of the kingdom of heaven. You won't go in yourselves, and you keep others from going in.**
>
> **You Pharisees and teachers of the Law of Moses are in for trouble! You're nothing but show-offs. You travel over land and sea to win one follower. And when you have done so, you make that person twice as fit for hell as you are.**
>
> **You are in for trouble! You are supposed to lead others, but you are blind. You teach that it doesn't matter if a person swears by the temple. But you say that it does matter if someone swears by the gold in the temple.**

You blind fools! Which is greater, the gold or the temple that makes the gold sacred?

You also teach that it doesn't matter if a person swears by the altar. But you say that it does matter if someone swears by the gift on the altar.

Are you blind? Which is more important, the gift or the altar that makes the gift sacred?

Anyone who swears by the altar also swears by everything on it.

And anyone who swears by the temple also swears by God, who lives there.

To swear by heaven is the same as swearing by God's throne and by the one who sits on that throne.

You Pharisees and teachers are show-offs, and you're in for trouble! You give God a tenth of the spices from your garden, such as mint, dill, and cumin. Yet you neglect the more important matters of the Law, such as justice, mercy, and faithfulness. These are the important things you should have done, though you should not have left the others undone either.

You blind leaders! You strain out a small fly but swallow a camel.

You Pharisees and teachers are show-offs, and you're in for trouble! You wash the outside of your cups and dishes, while inside there is nothing but greed and selfishness.

You blind Pharisee! First clean the inside of a cup, and then the outside will also be clean.

You Pharisees and teachers are in for trouble! You're nothing but show-offs. You're like tombs that have been whitewashed. On the outside they are beautiful, but inside they are full of bones and filth.

That's what you are like. Outside you look good, but inside you are evil and only pretend to be good.

You Pharisees and teachers are nothing but show-offs, and you're in for trouble! You build monuments for the prophets and decorate the tombs of good people.

And you claim that you would not have taken part with your ancestors in killing the prophets.

But you prove that you really are the relatives of the ones who killed the prophets.

So keep on doing everything they did.

You are nothing but snakes and the children of snakes! How can you escape going to hell?

I will send prophets and wise people and experts in the Law of Moses to you. But you will kill them or nail them to a cross or beat them in your meeting places or chase them from town to town.

That's why you will be held guilty for the murder of every good person, beginning with the good man Abel. This also includes Barachiah's son Zechariah, the man you murdered between the temple and the altar.

I can promise that you people living today will be punished for all these things!

Jerusalem, Jerusalem! Your people have killed the prophets and have stoned the messengers who were sent to you. I have often wanted to gather your people, as a hen gathers her chicks under her wings. But you wouldn't let me.

And now your temple will be deserted.

You won't see me again until you say, "Blessed is the one who comes in the name of the Lord." (Matthew 23)

How should we deal with the spirit of Religion?

First, pray.

Prayer is the rain that softens the driest and hardest of soil. If there is a failure to change hearts on this, leaders must remove those through whom a spirit of Religion is operating from every position of influence, until there is a heart change. It would be more dangerous not to, and the costs will become considerable. Without repentance, relationships will decay and cause fractures in the church or organization.

With every ministry done, there are three main steps to follow:

Repent;
Renounce; and
Break.

Here is a **sample prayer** you might choose to use.

"Father God, creator of heaven and earth, I come to you in the name of Jesus Christ your Son. I come as a sinner seeking forgiveness and cleansing from all sins committed against you, and others made in your image. I honor my earthly father and mother and all of my ancestors of flesh and blood, and of the spirit by adoption and godparents, but I utterly turn away from and renounce all their sins and iniquities. I forgive all my ancestors for the effects of their sins on me and my children. I confess and renounce all of my own sins, known or unknown. I renounce and rebuke Satan and every spiritual power of his affecting me and my family, in the name of Jesus Christ.

True Holy Creator God, in the name of the True Lord Jesus Christ, in accordance with Jude 8-10; Psalm 82:1 and 2 Chronicles 18, I request you to move aside all Celestial Beings, including Principalities, Powers and Rulers, and to forbid them to harass, intimidate or retaliate against me and all participants in this ministry today.

I also ask that you prevent these beings of whatever rank, to not be permitted to send any level of spiritual evil as retaliation against any of those here, or our families, our ministries, or possessions.

I renounce and annul every covenant made with Death by my ancestors or myself, including every agreement made with Sheol, and I renounce the refuge of lies and falsehoods that have been hidden behind.

In the name of Jesus Christ, I repent and renounce every opening, known or unknown, that I or my ancestors have given to every spirit of Religion in my family line.

I repent and renounce every spirit of Religion or religious spirit, and every work of darkness connected with it.

I repent for not fully receiving your love, compassion, mercy, grace

and forgiveness; and I renounce any belief that You, Lord, are distant and judgemental. I choose to embrace all aspects of Your character and to intimately know you.

In the name of Jesus Christ, I repent for allowing myself to be led by any other spirit than Your Holy Spirit.

I repent for relying on my own intellect in worship, praise, prayer, reading the Bible - God's Word, and spiritual warfare.

In the name of Jesus Christ, I repent and renounce all legalism, traditions and religious formulas, and participation in dead works, dullness to the things of God, and hardness of heart.

I now choose to invite the Holy Spirit to lubricate my heart with His oil, and make it pliable to accommodate all the things God wants for me.

I repent and renounce every man's opinion of me where this is different from the opinion of my Heavenly Father.

I repent and renounce all compromises, of the truth, of my integrity and of my purity.

I repent and renounce all compromises in my attitude towards sin. I repent and renounce my lack of transparency for covering sin, not confessing sin, for not receiving correction, for being defensive and quick to justify and rationalise my sin.

I repent and renounce all deception and hypocrisy; all pride, arrogance and self-righteousness.

I repent and renounce all comparison, judgement, criticism, gossip, jealousy, covetousness, and anger.

I repent and renounce all persecution and slander of those moving in the Holy Spirit, especially those leaders God had placed in authority over me.

I repent and renounce every act of rebellion that has reinforced the spirit of Religion in my life.

I choose now to have obedience to God and His Word as my attitude.

I choose to no longer partner with the same spirit which killed Jesus, and that continues to attempt to kill the work of the Holy Spirit today.

I come out of agreement with the enemies of the Most High God, and I choose to come into agreement with God my Father, with His Son Messiah Jesus Christ and the Holy Spirit.

In the name of Jesus Christ I now break every hex, curse, vow, every spell, incantation or ritual, every covenant, blood covenant, every sacrifice and blood sacrifice.

I break every ungodly soul-tie, and every generational tie in my family bloodline that does not honour the Holy Spirit and His works.

In the name of Jesus Christ, I now break every other legal right, known or unknown, for the spirit of Religion to stay in my life, or in my family's lives.

I speak now with the Body of Christ to every spirit of Religion, and we say to you we come against you in the name of the Lord Jesus Christ, we rebuke you in His name, and we refuse to allow you to steal our intimate relationship with our Lord Jesus Christ.

We refuse to allow you to kill the flow of the Holy Spirit in us, and in our congregations.

We refuse to allow you to destroy the anointing of the Holy Spirit through us.

We choose to receive the anointing to break the power of the spirit of Religion in the Church of the Lord Jesus Christ.

Now, dear Father God, I ask humbly for the blood of Jesus Christ, your Son and my Saviour, to cleanse me from all these sins I have confessed and renounced, to cleanse my spirit, my soul, my mind, my emotions and every part of my body which has been affected by these sins, in the name of Jesus Christ. I also ask to receive the perfect love of God which casts out all fear, in the name of the Lord Jesus Christ.

I ask you, Lord, to fill me with your Holy Spirit now according to the promises in your Word. I take to myself the whole armour of God in accordance with Ephesians Chapter Six, and rejoice in its protection as Jesus surrounds me and fills me with His Holy Spirit. I enthrone you, Lord Jesus, in my heart, for you are my Lord and my Savior, the source of eternal life. Thank you, Father God, for your mercy, your forgiveness and your love, in the name of Jesus Christ, Amen."

Chapter 9
Do Christians Ever Need Deliverance from Demons?

Dr. Derek Prince writes, *"At one time an official publication of a major denomination classified Don Basham and me as heretics because we were casting demons out of Christians. "What are we supposed to do?" I asked Don. "Leave the demons in them?" The charge against us was based, of course, on the assumption that Christians could never have demons that would need to be cast out. (Later this charge was apparently forgotten, because churches belonging to that denomination have since invited me to minister deliverance.)*

In more than thirty years, I have never heard or read a reasoned, scriptural presentation of the doctrinal position that Christians can never need deliverance from demons. Those who believe this, ...seem to consider it so obvious that it needs no support from Scripture. But the implications of such a position can be, to say the least, surprising."
("They Shall Expel Demons" by Dr. Derek Prince p 142)

Regarding the Demonic realm, please consider the following: James 4:7 instructs us to submit to God (first), then to resist the devil, and only then he will flee. This doesn't mean you will have a personal encounter with Satan himself, but one of his delegated underlings. If you aren't submitted to God the rest won't happen, and in all probability you will get attacked.

Dr. Prince received his last deliverance while much older than 60 years of age. He mentions this in one of his audio teachings. He knew he had something, and admitted he didn't know what it was, until someone had a Word of Knowledge at the YWAM base in Hawaii. He was set free immediately. So the possibility that other Christians may have a"Klingon" is very likely.

Chapter 10
As You Minister Deliverance

1. Be compassionate, not judgmental. The secret perversions of man's fallen nature will sometimes surprise you. "Therefore comfort each other and edify one another, just as you also are doing." (1 Thessalonians 5:11)

2. Require the believer to be uncompromising with the enemy and hate what God hates. Deuteronomy 7:1-2 says "When the Lord your God brings you into the land which you go to possess, and has cast out many nations before you, ... and when the Lord your God delivers them over to you, you shall conquer them and utterly destroy them. You shall make no covenant with them nor show mercy to them." Why did God tell them to do this? Because these nations were all demon-infested and we are not to make covenants with demonically-led people.

3. Have a listening ear as God identifies the root problem for you. Notice James 1:19... "Therefore, my beloved brethren, let every man be quick to hear, slow to speak, slow to anger." We have to learn to listen.

4. Be flexible in a variety of techniques or methods. "The heart of the prudent acquires knowledge, and the ear of the wise seeks knowledge." (Proverbs 18:15)

5. Use the Sword of the Spirit, the Word of God, as it described in Ephesians 6:17. The Sword of the Spirit is the offensive part of the Armor of God. But you must know the Word. For example, when there is fear, you must hit the enemy with 2 Timothy 1:7... **"For God has not given us a spirit of fear, but of Love and Power, and a Sound Mind."** Use the Word of God that comes against that spirit. If there is a spirit of weakness, then use Philippians 4:13... **"I can do all things through Jesus Christ who strengthens me."**

6. Don't Believe evil spirits. 1 John 4:1-3 says **"Beloved, do not believe every spirit, but test the spirits, whether they are of God;**

because many false prophets have gone out into the world. By this you know the Spirit of God: Every spirit that confesses that Jesus Christ has come in the flesh is of God, and every spirit that does not confess that Jesus Christ has come in the flesh is not of God. And this is the spirit of the Anti-christ, which you have heard was coming, and is now already in the world."

We always try to test the spirits. Even when we see great manifestations, which might indicate that a spirit is leaving, we want to make sure that the devil did not give false manifestations to try and fool us.

False Concepts & Half-Truths about Deliverance

Obstacles to Deliverance	Answers to Obstacles
1. Unbelief: There is no such thing as the devil or demons.	Jesus had a confrontation with the devil. Jesus defeated the devil by quoting Scripture. We are to do the same. (Luke 4:1-13)
2. Demons are real, but too powerful for us to confront.	Jesus gave us all the authority and power we need to over come demons. (Mark 16:17; Luke 10:19)
3. There should be deliverance, but it should be left to experts.	Any believer in Jesus can cast out demons. (Mark 16:17)
4. Christians cannot have demons.	This false view is based on a distorted understanding about the Omnipresence of God.
5. Demons have no activity in civilized countries. They are only active in remote countries where witchcraft and superstitions prevail.	The devil goes everywhere on the earth. (Job 2:2; 1 Peter 5:8)

6. If we cast out demons they will come back seven times worse.	Only if the stronger man, the Holy Spirit, is not in that person. After casting out demons, we invite the Holy Spirit to come in, & fill them. (1 John 4:4)
7. Deliverance must never be done in public.	Jesus did it in public. (Mark 1:23)
8. Deliverance is purely a matter of faith. We don't need to do any more than believe we are free.	Jesus said to cast them out. (Mark 16:17; Matthew 10:8)
9. Deliverance must occur with manifestations; e.g. screaming, fighting, etc.	No, demons usually come out by expelling your breath. (Luke 10:19; Luke 8:28-30)
10. Demonology and deliverance glorify the devil. We should just keep our minds on Jesus.	Anything done in the name of Jesus Christ, as He commanded, glorifies Jesus. (Mark 16;17)
11. Persons who get involved in deliverance suffer personal attacks from demons or Satan.	Luke 10:19 is the answer; **"Nothing shall hurt you."**
12. Jesus did it all for us. Since Jesus defeated the devil we can just forget about the devil.	That is what the devil would like us to believe. Jesus told us how to defeat the devil. Cast him out. (Mark 16:17) Then we are protected by the Blood of the Lamb, and the word of our testimony. (Revelation 12:11)

("Do's, Dont's, Failures & False Concepts abbreviated from "Manual for the Deliverance Worker" by late Frank Marzullo Snr,)

Chapter 11
How to Minister to Yourself

A Missionary veteran of some 50 years in Guatemala, Norman Parish, outlines the following to minister to oneself. This should also be useful to those doing such ministry with others.

1. Seek to set aside a day or more to seek God in prayer and fasting. Try to shut out all outside distractions.

2. Let your pastor or elder know what you are planning to do, so they can assist you in case of need. Hopefully, they will have some understanding of (and better still, experience in) deliverance and spiritual warfare.

3. Honestly confess any known or besetting sin on your own life. Be strict on yourself. Don't try to justify your past failures or to blame them on someone else.

4. Confess the sins of your ancestors (please read Nehemiah 1:5,6 and Daniel 9:4-12, 16-19), asking God at the same time to nullify the effects of those sins upon your family line. If you suspect that you or your family is affected by an ancestral curse, by faith nullify its power over you. Any legal right or hold that the Devil might have over your life because of the sins of your ancestors needs to be cancelled out through the proper exercise of spiritual authority.

5. Begin to claim the freedom Christ has granted you through His death and resurrection. Speak directly to the demons that you believe are plaguing your life, oppressing your mind or disrupting your home. Name them and command them out of your personal life and home. Don't give up, no matter how fierce their opposition might be. Insist adamantly on their leaving. Don't be surprised if you feel certain physical or emotional reactions - such as a blinding headache, nausea, weakness, trembling, depression, crying, and so forth. If this happens, it only comes to prove that what you are doing is having a direct and devastating effect on the spirits that have kept you in bondage.

6. Demons many times leave through the respiratory tract (mouth and nose). As they leave, you might yawn, cough, belch, vomit, etc. Don't let this frighten you. In the course of your deliverance, you will begin to feel that a heavy burden is lifting off your heart and mind. You will feel light and clean inside. Don't stop short. Persist until you feel total release from whatever is oppressing you.

7. As your deliverance culminates, the Holy Spirit will bear testimony to your spirit that the Devil's influence or control in certain critical areas of your life has been abolished. Begin to praise and thank God for "the glorious liberty of the children of God." The final evidence that you have been set free from the Devil's grip is the noticeable change that will take place in your character, health, nerves, mental attitude, etc.

8. Demons always seek to regain the ground they have lost in your life (Matthew 12:43-45). You will always have to be on full alert (Matthew 26:41; 1 Peter 5:8), in order to ward off their attacks. There is no greater protection from the Devil's onslaughts than the fullness of the Spirit. If you have never received the Spirit's power, seek it earnestly by asking the Lord to fill you with or in the Holy Spirit (Acts 1:4,5,8; 2:4). If you have already had this glorious experience, then ask God daily to refill you (Ephesians 5:18). As you walk in the Spirit (Galatians 5:16,25; Romans 8:1,4), Satan's power over you will be nullified. That will enable you to live the victorious Christian life you have always yearned after. (Abbreviated from "Deliver Thyself" by Norman Parish, pps 55-58, published by Jubilee)

God sets us free so we can serve Him fruitfully. A self-centered life probably caused our problem in the first place, so we need to change our priorities now if we want to stay free.

Chapter 12
What Happens Next?

When people go to hospital for surgery, the nursing staff assist with recovery, by ensuring the patient can look after themselves to a sufficient degree.

Deliverance is no different, in many respects. The following guidelines should prove helpful. As the Gibson's stated in their book on deliverance *"Every blessing of God is conditional. Our co-operation is essential."* ("Evicting Demonic Squatters & Breaking Bondages" by Noel & Phyl Gibson, p 189.) It is most disappointing when people have been ministered to, and yet within days or weeks they have taken back the demons through bad choices, inadequate post-ministry help, or substandard ministry in the first place

The blessings of God come when we do ministry His way, led by the Holy Spirit and authorized by Jesus Christ, and with the wholehearted agreement of the person receiving ministry. There are too many people who come with a problem, and say words to the effect, *"Here's the problem, just fix it and don't bother me with the details."* Sin must be owned up to and repented of before we can fulfil God's requirements for freedom.

While most people receiving ministry will need some support and on-going encouragement, many can be given self-help things to do so they can grow and mature in their own spiritual walk. The goal is for the person to find freedom in Jesus Christ and the support of an accepting Christian fellowship so they no longer need further ministry.

1. Each day, make right choices so you can stay free. If you were set free from spirits of lust, such as pornography etc., then don't go on the web looking for more, and don't hang around porn books - get out of there. If you were set free from spirits of alcohol, don't hang around people who drink or places which serve it. Apply as the issues are appropriate. Do NOT play with deliberate sin.

2. Declare aloud in prayer daily your thanks to God for His freedom from the issue/s. "Thank you God for taking away my lust/anger/rejection, (whatever)."

3. Since the devil is a liar, as well as sneaky, expect him through the demons sent to control you to try and tempt you, and he will hope to snare you again in the same or similar sins. This will open you up to those spirits which were expelled to return, and bring their mates with them. Knowing this means making sure you don't open the door to them.

4. If you had been hearing voices prior to ministry, resist the temptation to converse with them, even if they seek to return. Just tell them to go, in the name and authority of Jesus, and declare aloud that you are clean because of the blood of Jesus shed at Calvary.

5. One of Satan's most effective methods is to bring condemnation. Don't allow anything to come between you and Jesus. Refuse to accept guilt, condemnation or doubt, because "There is, therefore, now no condemnation for those who are in Christ Jesus, because through Christ the law of the spirit of life set me free from the law of sin and death." (Romans 8:1-2) Make this a daily proclamation verbally, and write it up and place it where you see it often - perhaps on top of your mirror in your bedroom or bathroom. There is another Scripture that you could also proclaim and write up - "So if the Son (Jesus) sets you free, you shall be free indeed." (John 8:36)

6. If you do fall into temptation and sin in the area/s you have received ministry in, immediately confess this to God and renounce any attempt for evil spirits to come and re-inhabit you.

7. Invite the Holy Spirit to enable you to obey Him all day long, to make you into the image of Jesus Christ, to change in ways that would please your Heavenly Father. While you are engaged with God, Satan won't be able to dial your number.

8. Make time daily to read and study your Bible, and to converse with God frequently. Don't spend all your time asking for things, thank

Him for what He has been doing in your life, and by faith thank Him for what He is going to continue to do in and through you. Look up, study and write up the following Scriptures as you grow spiritually: Joshua 1:8; Psalm 119:9-11; 2 Timothy 2:15

9. Learn about the Armor of God, and learn how to wear this spiritually all the time (Ephesians 6). Jesus prayed for your protection in John 17:5; and taught His disciples to protect themselves. (Matthew 6:13) Jesus has attested and approved each article for your protection. (Hebrews 2:17-18) So you would be foolish to neglect these.

10. Train yourself in thankfulness and praise of God. Praise disturbs the enemy. Never be ungrateful for what God has done for you. Satan fears the praising followers of Jesus Christ. Check out Psalm 103:2 and Colossians 1:20, and apply these regularly.

11. God will never abandon you, so you are never alone. He has never broken a promise yet. Check out Hebrews 13:5-6, Matthew 28:20, and Romans 8:38-39. Write these out, and display them around your house or living space. These are true, and you can stake your life on them.

12. If it becomes necessary, break friendships that will lead you into sin, (see James 4:4). Good friends become a blessing to each other. But there are many people who become parasitic, draining the spiritual life out of us. Avoid them. Real friends are heading to the same destination - God's will.

Appendix 1
Talking with Demons

This vexed issue keeps raising its head from time to time. This testimony from a pastor involved in the Deliverance ministry has very pertinent points worth sharing.

Don Rogers Testimony

"When I first began to minister to the demonized over 30 years ago, all I knew to do for the people I was ministering to was to pray for their bondage to be broken. At the time this was a new type of ministry for me and I had no training to equip me for it. There was very little literature available and what was available was not always good.

As I relied on prayer, the cases usually took a long time before we got breakthroughs. During this time I was asking God for wisdom and guidance, so that I could be more effective in serving Him. As time went on, I learned that some in deliverance were interrogating demons to provide the information needed to deal with them effectively. I remember that Jesus had asked the Gadarene demoniac his name and he said it was "Legion."

So for a few years I began to interrogate demons. As I did so, their manifestations became more prominent. Often they would come to the surface and I could see their individual characters in the eyes and facial expressions of the victims. They were often vehement, spewing forth intimidating and profane language directed against me and my family. There was also considerable violent behavior. During this time, there was something very unsettling in my spirit about what was happening. God had given me grace not to yield to fear, but still I believed that something was wrong. I knew that demons were liars by nature and that they served the father of lies (John 8:44). Even though I was growing in my understanding as to how to exercise Christ's authority against them, I knew in my heart often the best I was going to get out of them were "half-truths" which are more misleading than overt lies. I also began to realize that when Jesus asked for the Gadarene demoniac's name, it was for our benefit in understanding the magnitude of some demonizations. Jesus did not have to ask for his name in order to deal with him. The Holy Spirit guided Him in all things.

I began to ask God a lot of questions. I wanted to know how to be a better servant. I desire to be more effective against the enemy, not giving him even an inch. I was concerned about how other deliverance ministries seemed to be focused on demonic manifestations and seemed to relish in them in order to receive peoples' validation concerning what they were doing.

My background was formed in conservative evangelicalism. I was taught that many of the sign gifts were not for today. I didn't realize it at the time, but what I was really being taught was that God had changed! There was a strong appreciation to rely upon the word of God, but often man's theology got in the way. I began to see a number of people to whom I was ministering have their spiritual gifts released and made operational. Many would even assist in their own deliverance, telling me what the enemy was doing to resist me. The sessions became more powerful in the Lord than ever before. I went back to the word of God with new insights and came to the realization that what I had been taught was in error. So, I asked a couple of very gifted people, who apparently were called to ministry, to assist me. Immediately, the effectiveness of the ministry was raised. Over the years, in my association with gifted people, my own gifts have come to the forefront and been enhanced as well.

When spiritual gifts began to be used in our ministry, I ceased to interrogate demons any longer. When I took this step of faith, the Lord began to show me why He had directed me in this matter. Unknowingly, when I had relied upon interrogation of the enemy, I was giving the enemy more power to resist me. By commanding them to communicate with me, I was giving them control of parts of the victims' brains, especially the speech centre. I was giving the enemy the opportunity to demonstrate his vileness and provided him with the opportunity to deceive and resist.

I believe in a confrontational ministry, but only to the point that I confront them in the power of the Lord. I made a covenant with the

Lord. I told Him that I wanted to be the best that I could be in serving Him and bringing credibility to this type of ministry. I did not believe that continuous and regular demonic manifestations during ministry was honoring to Him or to a ministry that serves Him. I asked Him to shut down this type of activity or enable us to do so. I desired that this ministry have the witness of the Holy Spirit behind it, not the witness of demons and their activity. I didn't need the approval of people, only the Lord.

Immediately, the spiritual atmosphere of our ministry changed. It was transformed into a very calm and gentle ministry, but very powerful. Any demonic manifestations were quickly shut down. Demons were immediately silenced. Not only were deliverances enhanced, they were done more quickly and healing of the demonic destruction became more prominent. Needless to say, as soon as we started to rely completely on the Holy Spirit, the enemy counterattacked with vengeance. My own church asked me to leave, because I was using spiritual gifts in my ministry. Other churches and Christian friends began to slander me and blackball me and treat me like a heretic. When I visited church elder boards to explain the biblical basis for our change of ministry, they did not want to examine the Bible with me, because I was already in conflict with their theology. What does a person do when there is an unjustified, widespread activity to discredit them? Letters were being sent to other churches to inform them of the error in which I had become involved. There is only one thing you can do; trust the Lord. I said to the Lord, that He knew my heart. I was relying upon Him to be my protector. There was no other means that I could protect myself, without relying upon the flesh. So, I trust in Him to take me through the fire and today our ministry is widely respected. We are even in a referral network of Christian psychologists and psychiatrists. Isn't our God great!!

I mentioned that healing became more prominent in our ministry. I came to realize that deliverance and healing were inseparable. God wants to heal and restore what the enemy has sought to destroy. I count it a privilege to see God do miracles constantly before my eyes. Often God starts working upon the individual even before I start to minister. When people enter our ministry office, they sense the presence of the

Lord. Many have seen, with their spiritual gifts, the two angels that God has assigned to me as I lay hands on the victims and minister deliverance and healing. Sometimes I sense their presence, but I have never seen them. They are there to assist me and to provide protection. I often call upon God to send in angels to assist me when I run into stiff resistance. They not only serve God's people, but they are harvesters of that which is evil. Upon occasion there has been a visible manifestation of the tug of war between these two forces.

I find that God is using our ministry to give people breakthroughs and an opportunity for a new start in life. Much of what is accomplished happens after they leave us. God is not interested in glorifying us. He wants to strengthen and enhance their intimacy with Him. They should not continue to depend upon us. In the weeks that follow, new freedoms are introduced into their lives as they are ready to receive them. They are accountable to be obedient to what God shows them and asks of them. We challenge them to fortify their minds with the word of God, especially His promises. We have stacks of letters recounting the dramatic changes that take place in the 4 - 6 weeks that follow. Healing continues and sometimes a measure of deliverance continues.

Our ministry is not meant to be a magic wand that relieves people of their problems, so that they can go back and lead their lives as usual. As we initially screen the people that come to us, their motivation for seeking help is an important consideration. God has called us to challenge them to become disciples of the Lord, to be accountable for their lives before Him. There can be no compromise with the world or with the enemy. No one can serve two masters. They have to be honest with themselves, with others and with the Lord. Those who have been set free will remain free as long as they trust and obey the Lord. If they choose to consistently yield to the enemy or the world and rebel against God, they will in all likelihood go back into bondage. The choice is theirs." (by Don Rogers, "Spiritual Warfare Ministries, 1998)

I also came across the following statement provided by a friend after he had been searching the Internet for material on this subject.

A Word of Warning to Deliverance Ministries

We often wondered why many deliverance ministers oftentimes seem to have such personal and/or health problems; yet, they are doing the work of Jesus Christ.

The answer may lie in the fact that most, if not all, feel they have to speak to the demons they are expelling - find out their name, what they do, how they inhabited or find their victims - how did the possession come about?

For instance, in the Roman Catholic Church, one of the rituals is to force the demon to give his name and how did it come to choose this particular person.

Roman Catholic priests performing an "exorcism" ritual are often attacked by the victim's residing demon or demons when they begin to converse with them.

The demons can cause heart attacks, strokes, or other health problems then or later, when confrontation is made verbally. It is an awesome thing.

In fact, Father John O'Connor (not Cardinal John O'Connor) said that because the energy loss from a true exorcist is so great, a Roman Catholic exorcist lives only about 15 years after he is deeply involved in this. However, there are exceptions and no one really knows why some live much longer.

He further says the hatred from the demon(s) is so horrendous that it literally drains the priests doing the "exorcism."

Furthermore, many priests tend to believe the demons when they are being confronted verbally. The accusations and accounts the demoniac gives about the possession, about the personal life of the individual possessed, and about the individuals doing or assisting in the exorcism are more often than not taken as truth by the small group assisting or performing the ritual.

Some facts may be true, to rivet the individuals in the small room where the "exorcism" is being performed. Then, may follow total falsehoods. This is reason for extreme caution.

In our research and studies, we have found one definitive and one very strong reason why one in the deliverance ministry should not permit the demon to speak.

Regarding "Exorcism"

The point has been made elsewhere in the book, but needs repeating here: "Exorcism" is a pre-Christian magic ritual that puts demons into people to suppress weaker demons. That's not freedom! Christians do "Deliverance," not "Exorcism." Roman Catholics, and some others, use the term wrongly.

Faculty of Paris Theologians

"In the year 1610 a committee of learned theologians had discussed the admissibility of diabolic evidence and issued the following authoritative decision:

We, the undersigned Doctors of the Faculty of Paris, touching certain questions which have been proposed to us, are of the opinion that one must never admit to the accusation of demons, still less must one exploit exorcisms for the purpose of discovering a man's faults or for determining if he is a magician, and we are further of the opinion that, even if the said exorcisms should have been applied in the presence of the Holy Sacrament, with the devil forced to swear an oath (which is a ceremony we do not at all approve), one must not for all that give any credit to his words, the devil being always a liar and the 'Father of Lies.'

Furthermore, the devil is man's sworn enemy, and is therefore ready to endure all the torments of exorcism for the sake of doing harm to a single soul. If the devil's evidence were admitted, the most virtuous people would be in the greatest danger; for it is precisely against these Satan rages most violently.

Wherefore St. Thomas (Book 22, Question 9, Article 22) maintains with the authority of St. Chrysostom, Daemoni, Etiam Vera Dicenti, Non Est Credendum. [The devil must not be believed, even when he tells the truth].

We must follow the example of Christ, who imposed silence on the demons even when they spoke truth, by calling him the Son of God.

Energy Deprivation
Being in the presence of demons is horrendous, such that one must also take caution to have eaten enough complete protein for several days to several weeks prior to the encounter.

This demonic presence literally drains the biochemistry and regenerative powers of the deliverance minister. This is why, we believe, so many Catholic priests and Protestant deliverance ministers complain about the tremendous exhaustion after a deliverance." (Source: www.tex-is.net/users/csbrocato/deliver/html.)

My View

Some who support this dangerous practice of interviewing demons quote Mark 5 where Jesus had a "conversation" with Legion, the spiritual strongman controlling the demoniac of the Gaderenes. I note, however, the demons spoke first: Jesus didn't initiate this conversation, but he finished it fairly quickly. Dr. John Sandford has an interesting insight into Mark 5 and Legion. John said that Jesus was testing (for our benefit) whether the man was in control, or if the demons had total control. When the control was claimed by the demons' spokesman, "Legion," Jesus exercised faith for their eviction and the man's deliverance since he couldn't do that for himself.

Let me summarize the issue of conversations or interviews with demons. Demons cannot be relied on to tell the whole truth - they are 'evil' spirits after all, and under the control of Satan whom Jesus declared to be the Father of Lies. It seems to me, and I have asked many Christian leaders involved in the Deliverance ministry, that information from a demon is questionable, a poor substitute when compared with information from the Holy Spirit (which Jesus declared is the “Spirit of Truth” - John 14:17; 16:13). On my reading of the Scriptures, interviewing demons is called “Mediumship” and invokes the curse of God. On the above basis, speaking with demons (other than evicting them) is both sinful and unnecessary.

Appendix 2
The Deliverance Miracles of Jesus

Since we are commanded in Scripture to copy what Jesus did, let us look briefly at the miracles of Jesus, and you will see how often these involve healing and deliverance. Of the 37 recorded miracles of Jesus, there were eight expulsions of demonic spirits. (To save space I have provided the references only. You might care to use these as an outline for a home-group study, discussion and practice.)

As you will have noticed, many of these were recorded in more than one of the Gospels. It is possible some miracles recorded by more than one of the Gospel writers may be about different events, although there seems enough evidence to group some of these situations as the same event but recorded with a variety of details by each of the writers.

Mark 1:23-28; Luke 4:33-37 - Jesus expels an "unclean spirit" from a man in a synagogue. Jesus didn't get into a chat with the demon - with a simple command, the evil spirit was gone.

Matthew 8:14-15; Mark 1:30-31; Luke 4:38-39 - Simon Peter's mother-in-law had a fever, but when Jesus rebuked it, the fever left. When Jesus simply healed a person with an non-demonic illness, He commanded the healing without using the term "rebuke." His use of the term "rebuke" is to do with removing the demonic. This is an example.

Matthew 8:16-17; Mark 1:32-34; Luke 4:40-41 - Jesus healed all the sick, cast out demonic spirits, and in Mark "He did not allow the demons to speak."

Matthew 12:22-23; Luke 11:14 - Jesus expels a demon which caused a man to be blind and mute. This resulted in healing.

Matthew 9:32-35 - A mute demon-possessed man is brought to Jesus. The man spoke following the casting out of the demon.

Matthew 15:21-28; Mark 7:25-29 - After some discussion, Jesus heals the distant daughter of the persistent Syro-Phoenician woman. The girl's sickness was caused by an unclean spirit.

Matthew 17:14-21; Mark 9:17-29; Luke 9:38-42 - A child is healed of muteness and epilepsy when the demon causing it is cast out by Jesus.

Luke 13:11-17 - Jesus heals a woman who had be bent over with a spirit of infirmity for eighteen years. Another Sabbath healing.

The full list of all the miracles of Jesus may be located in our Biblical Healing Training Manual - see list of titles by the same author.

Appendix 3
Soul-ties/Ungodly Relationship Bonds

These occur in a number of ways. The concept of soul ties has only recently been understood and the fruit of this has resulted in real freedom in those who have broken ungodly soul-ties.

The key term regarding soul-ties is "covenant." One example is found in Mark 10:7-8.

> **'For this reason a man shall leave his father and mother and be joined to his wife, 'and the two shall become one flesh'; so then they are no longer two but one flesh. Mark 10:7-8.**

The Biblical word that describes this bond that takes place is "cleave." The Greek word is kollao and it means to glue or cement your soul to another person's soul. Vine's Dictionary of New Testament Words gives us the following definition: "KOLLAO, to join fast together, to glue, cement... (from Kolla, glue)."

When we know that the Biblical word cleave is the Greek word kollao and that it comes from the Greek word kolla, that means glue, it is easier to understand the spiritual damage that takes place as the result of sexual sin.

Another example includes David and Jonathan recorded in 1 Samuel 18:1-4. The King James Version says **"Their souls were knit together,"** as a result of this covenant. There is unreserved commitment. These are Godly soul-ties - a righteous covenant. Ungodly soul-ties are frequently sexual in nature, but not always. Let's look at some examples.

- Bikers make a covenant with "brothers" in a gang.
- New Agers make a covenant to worship mother earth/creation then Father God the Creator.
- Freemasons make ungodly covenants with lodge "brothers" and the "GAOTU."
- Many people make ungodly covenant with religious organizations and this isn't limited just to cults.

- Some non-sexual parent/child relationships can invoke ungodly soul-ties when there are inappropriate or unbalanced relationships involving control issues.

We can also see the soul tie at work in the Old Testament Scriptures.

> **Now Dinah the daughter of Leah, whom she had borne to Jacob, went out to see the daughters of the land. And when Shechem the son of Hamor the Hivite, prince of the country, saw her, he took her and lay with her, and violated her. His soul was strongly attracted to Dinah the daughter of Jacob, and he loved the young woman and spoke kindly to the young woman. (Genesis 34:1-3)**

> **But King Solomon loved many foreign women, as well as the daughter of Pharaoh: women of the Moabites, Ammonites, Edomites, Sidonians, and Hittites from the nations of whom the LORD had said to the children of Israel, "You shall not intermarry with them, nor they with you. Surely they will turn away your hearts after their gods." Solomon clung to these in love. And he had seven hundred wives, princesses, and three hundred concubines; and his wives turned away his heart For it was so, when Solomon was old, that his wives turned his heart after other gods; and his heart was not loyal to the LORD his God, as was the heart of his father David. (1 Kings 11:1-4)**

Having said all this, the primary area of ungodly soul-ties is sexually based and stems from fornication, adultery, or homosexuality. In terms of ministry required, the best description I can give here is that an ungodly Soul-tie is a powerful bond between two persons, or a person and an object, that is empowered by an evil spirit or demon.

The keys to freedom from an ungodly soul-tie is firstly repentance before God for the sin or inappropriate relationship; followed by forgiveness to any other parties involved, including forgiving oneself; and then cutting the spiritual tie between you and that other person or persons or object, and then covering the ends of the soul-tie with the blood of Jesus Christ so they may never reconnect. Demons will try to bring the temptation to rejoin the ends through sinful activities.

Appendix 4
Suggested Prayer for Deliverance

(Following repentance and the declaration of faith in the Lordship of Jesus Christ, and the atoning work of His blood at Calvary. Remember the person's dignity, especially if others may be watching or you are in a public place.)

In the name of the Lord Jesus Christ of Nazareth, I command every evil spirit to depart from this person (name the person), you will leave on their natural breath now.

Your legal ground for being in _________ has been renounced and God has forgiven him/her. I forbid you to manifest, now, go immediately to the dry places, touching and harming no-one on the way, there to remain awaiting your judgement by the Lord Jesus Christ. You are forbidden to return to this person or any other human being, in the name of Jesus Christ of Nazareth.

Suggested Prayer for Breaking Ungodly Soul ties

Heavenly Father, I come to you in the name of the Lord Jesus Christ of Nazareth, your one and only Son, I confess, as sin, my involvement in sexual fornication and immorality. I repent of each of these ungodly relationships and ask for your forgiveness. I now receive your forgiveness according to your Word in 1 John 1:9.

Lord Jesus Christ of Nazareth I forgive _________ (the other party) and release them from all unforgiveness, bitterness, resentment,________, _________, (wait on the Holy Spirit to reveal anything else that may be hidden in your heart). I ask you Lord Jesus Christ to have mercy on them and reveal yourself to them that they too might be saved.

In the name and the authority of the Lord Jesus Christ of Nazareth, Holy Spirit please come with the Sword of the Spirit, the Word of God and the Blood of Jesus Christ and destroy all bondages and ungodly soul ties (sexual, spiritual, generational, blood oaths, blood covenants, blood dedications, blood ties and all other bondages between (to and from) _________ and _________ (the other party or perpetrator) and all demonic entities including all familiar spirits, unclean spirits, spirits of perversity; to and from all animals, places, situations, circumstances and events, breaking and destroying them once and for all into the blood of the Lord Jesus Christ of Nazareth.

Lord Jesus Christ of Nazareth I ask that all residue including any body fluids from any of these individuals be gathered up and removed from my spirit, soul and body and destroyed in the blood of Jesus Christ. I ask now for complete cleansing of my spirit, soul and body through the blood of Jesus from all defilement from these sins.

Holy Spirit, I ask that any parts of me that are held captive anywhere else would be set free, and returned to me washed, cleansed and purified in the blood of Jesus. Also any parts of ________ (other party) would be set free from me and return to them washed cleansed and purified in the blood of Jesus. Thank you, Lord Jesus Christ of Nazareth, that I have been set free from these ungodly soul ties which may no longer be used by the enemy to afflict me or my loved ones. I break off all the effects of these generational iniquities from me and my children. Please fill me afresh with your Holy Spirit, Lord Jesus Christ. Amen

About the Author:

Selwyn R. Stevens,

Ph.D.; D.Min.; M.I.S.D.M.; M.E.A.C.M.

is the President of Jubilee Resources International Inc. a New Zealand-based educational and religious organization involved in informing and equipping Christians of all denominations how to reach the lost and deceived in cults, the occult and secret societies such as Freemasonry. Author of over 35 books (and co-author of two), including twelve Best Sellers, an International Speaker (on five continents) and ordained minister. Dr. Stevens is a third-generation preacher, and has been involved in various Christian groups, and also maintains an active interest in national and world affairs and politics. Dr. Stevens is a Foundation Member of the International Society of Deliverance Ministers, founded by Dr. C. Peter Wagner and convened by Dr. William Sudduth of Virginia, USA; and Apostolic Overseer of the Alliance of African Christian Churches & Ministries based in Zambia. Regular Facebook and e-mail teaching and mentoring is also provided to many Christian leaders across Africa, Asia, Caribbean & Latin America, resulting in tens of thousands being equipped for service to the Kingdom of God.

About Jubilee Resources International

God's commission for Jubilee Resources International is based on Ezekiel 33:1-9, and Luke 4:18-21. According to the Bible, Jubilee years were times of restitution. Debts were cancelled, slaves set free, families reunited and lost or forfeited inheritances restored. Every year was prophetic of the ministry of Jesus Christ. The Jubilee was proclaimed on the basis of the work of the High Priest on the Day of Atonement - so Jesus Christ's liberating ministry is founded on His atoning work. Jesus began His public ministry by reading the passage from the prophet Isaiah (Luke 4:18-21). All the liberties of the Jubilee year are now available to us through the redemptive work of Jesus Christ at Calvary, and we all have the responsibility to preach this Gospel of Redemption and Restoration to full Relationship with Yahweh/Father God. When Yeshua/Jesus Christ returns, God's people will be totally free from all sin, sickness and disease, death and curse. The Biblical Jubilee will then be fully realized.

Resources in print book, eBook, audio & video formats are available in English, with paper & eBooks in Spanish, German, French, Italian, Portuguese-Brazil, Polish, Russian, Dutch, Swedish, Danish, Finnish, Hungarian, Romanian, Slovak, Czech, Greek, Afrikaans & Tagalog, with other languages pending.

Additional Resources Available by Selwyn R. Stevens

Dealing with Curses & Generational Iniquities. This teaching offers hope for all Christians that they can be released into the blessings of God and forever leave behind iniquities and curses that have kept them captive, perhaps their whole families for generations. This explains the twelve major curses that people may have operating in their families, and what to do about them. It also includes new material on the curses over Scottish, English, Irish, Welsh and Scandinavian people, plus many other national and ethnic groups. This teaching has been taught in several nations with much fruit for personal, family and community liberty. Best Seller
Book, E-book, MP4 & DVD

Dealing with Demons: *Insights into evil spiritual influences.* This popular teaching provides outstanding insights regarding evil spiritual influences that exist in the world in which we live today, and then goes further to show us what to do about it. Best Seller
Book, E-book, MP4 & DVD

Insights into Martial Arts, Tai Ch'i TM & Yoga. Much of the western world has seen an explosion of these practices. For many, their involvement has became close to a religion, adopting belief systems, mind sets and practises inconsistent with the teachings of the Bible. Best Seller
Book, E-book, MP4 & DVD

Treated or Tricked - Alternative Health Therapies Diagnosed. Many people are now trying Alternative Health Therapies. This book explains the various medical & spiritual healing methods; investigates whether the "Energy/Life Force" is scientific or spiritual; and describes almost 80 different Alternative Therapies, from Aromatherapy to Zone therapies. Also examines reasons why some are not healed & how to overcome these failures Biblically. Co-authored with Dr. Badu Bediako, (former Assoc. Professor of BioChemistry.) Best Seller
Book, E-book, MP4 & DVD

How to Recognize the Voice of God. How does God communicate to His people? How will you know when it is Him speaking to you? This very practical teaching has already helped many.
Book & DVD

Raising a Blessed Generation. The goals of this teaching are three-fold:
Goal 1: To understand what Blessing is and the Power it has for our lives today;
Goal 2: To Identify and Recover any missed blessings in my own life;
Goal 3: To Begin to Learn How to Bless others, especially our children & grandchildren! Identity and gender confusion is caused by the failure of parents & grandparents to speak identity and destiny into the young ones. Best Seller
Book, E-book, MP4 & DVD

Daniel and the Star Chasers. The counterfeit of Astrology has hidden what God wanted His people to know about the Gospel message in the stars. Daniel taught that truth to the Magi of Asia, and that nearly caused the War of the Continents half a millennium later. Only in recent decades has mankind had the technology to uncover what the Magi saw. Following Daniel's instructions, they went to see the King of Kings and submit their kingdoms and empires to His.
Book, E-book, MP4 & DVD

The Christian Life & the Role of the Fivefold Ministry. The Christian church is being increasingly side-lined in social debate. Have we ceased to be the Salt and Light commanded by Jesus Christ? The Solution: become real Christians! But what does that entail? Then, how are Christians to be governed? God provided the Fivefold ministry to do that. What does that look like? Best Seller
Book, E-book, MP4 & DVD

Help! The Sheep are Escaping: Understanding the Exodus From Church to God's Ecclesia. For most Christians in the West, "church" isn't working! The Old Wineskin cannot compete any longer, as God raises up His New Wineskin to fulfil His end-time purposes. The solution is for "church" to become Ecclesia and for participation with appropriate equipping, releasing and accountability.
Book, E-book, MP4 & DVD

Biblical Healing Training Manual. This thorough examination of Biblical physical healing is the result of many years of experience as well as training under some of the world's best Bible teachers. There are many "How To's", practical prayer and ministry guidelines, reasons why some aren't healed, and what we can do about them, etc. Hundreds have been healed, & many congregations have been empowered to commence regular Healing services with Christ-glorifying results. Best Seller
Book, E-book, MP4 & DVD

Fatal Faith - the Cult Counterfeit of Christianity. This book explains how cults develop and what patterns to avoid. Key Christian and Cult beliefs are compared with the main active cults. How to handle door-knockers, cult exiting, pre-cult spiritually-abusive churches; and how to protect young people from cults. Major ancient & modern heresies examined. Best Seller. *Book, E-book*

The New Age - the Old Lie in a New Package. New Age & Bible beliefs and practices compared, including Reincarnation and Past lives, Astrology, the New Age pseudo Messiah, Self-worship & our Deity-potential. Energy/ Life Forces are examined, and the occult involvement of most holistic health gurus. Best Seller *Book, E-book*

Discerning the Past to See the End Times: *Islam's Role in the Return of Jesus*. The statue in Nebuchadnezzar's dream, interpreted by Daniel, gives us a clear picture of the various empires that have sought domination of the Middle East and beyond. World events circle around this area of vital interest to God and His people. The Bible is a Middle Eastern book, not a European or American book. The context of the empires of the statue give us vital clues about the Empire of the Beast to come! Best Seller *Book, E-book, MP4 & DVD*

Signs & Symbols: Cult, New Age & Occult Insignias & What They Mean. From Ananda Marga, Anarchy, & Ankhs, to Yin & Yang, Yoga & Zodiacs. By popular demand this book has a brief explanation & a Biblical comparison with dozens of insignias. 7th Edition, newly revised. Best Seller *Book, E-book*

How to Minister to Change Lives and Communities. This comprehensive & practical training manual is for those who want to do effective ministry. This can include end-of-service and small-group ministry. Topics include Understanding the Spiritual Realm; Empowerment to Serve; Healing of the Body, & the Soul; Deeper Ministry by appointment & referral; & Biblical blessings to release identity and destiny. Best Seller *Book, E-book, MP4 & DVD*

The Bible 101. A teaching manual introducing the Bible, explaining clearly it's purposes, origins, history, inspiration, symbolism, translations & versions, moving from milk to meat, study helps, rules of interpretation, and how to study it to get the best understanding. *Book, E-book, & MP4*

Insights into Dying, Death & the Destination Options. This teaching has been providing comfort to many people who have been uncertain of their eternal future. This Biblical approach to a frequently misunderstood issue brings hope with joy, or the timely opportunity to make a crucial correction. *Book, E-book, & MP4*

Unmasking Freemasonry - Removing the Hoodwink. Written primarily for the wives & families of Masons to explain the curses brought on themselves and their families through the oaths; then learn how to deal with the effects. History & structure are explained simply. A Past Master who read this book immediately resigned from his Lodge. The prayer guidelines from this book are being used by many ministries worldwide. 7th edition with endorsement by C. Peter Wagner. Best Seller
Book, E-book, MP4 & DVD

Unmasking Mormonism - Who are the Latter-day Saints? Learn about LDS founder Joseph Smith on whose credentials this cult fails Bible tests, the Book of Mormon hoax, Mormon polytheism, true & false priesthood & authority. This book has caused many Mormons to cancel their baptisms & leave to seek the genuine Jesus Christ - the One from the Bible. Best Seller
Book, E-book, MP4 & DVD

Unmasking the Watchtower - Who are the Jehovah's Witnesses? This asks the questions many J.W.'s are being expelled for daring to ask! Check out the changeable prophecies and man-made doctrines of the Watchtower, the authoritarian leaders & their use of Mind-Control & manipulation of members, how to know the One True God, and how you can witness to and pray for a J.W. effectively. Best Seller
Book, E-book, MP4 & DVD

Rome's Anathemas: Insights into the Papal Pantheon. This vital book investigates Constantine's divorce of the Jewish roots of the Christian faith and its replacement with paganism; the Council of Trent rejected the Biblical basis of Luther's Reformation and cursed all who disagreed with them. In John, we read of the marriage feast at Cana. Realizing that the wine was gone and that she herself could not do anything, Mary tells Jesus, because He is the only One who could do something. Mary then gives the stewards her last recorded words and only command - one that we must consider for us to be saved. Mary said, *"Whatever He say to you, do it!"*
Book, E-book, MP4 & DVD

Additional Resources Available by Selwyn R. Stevens

www.jubileeresources.org (Webshop)
Plus comprehensive range of free tracts to download

Printed in Great Britain
by Amazon

43243411R00050